Allister & He
lore
Tessa & James.

Christmas 1981.

A CHILDHOOD
IN SCOTLAND

A CHILDHOOD IN SCOTLAND

Christian Miller

Illustrated by
RAY EVANS

JOHN MURRAY · LONDON

© Christian Miller 1979, 1981

First published 1981
by John Murray (Publishers) Ltd
50 Albemarle Street, London W1X 4BD

Typeset by Inforum Ltd, Portsmouth
Printed in Great Britain by
The Pitman Press, Bath

British Library Cataloguing in Publication Data
Miller, Christian
A childhood in Scotland.
1. Scotland — Social life and customs — 20th century
I.   Title
941.1082   DA826

ISBN 0-7195-3830-0

Foreword

A new generation, growing up in the castle, tells me that the ghosts have gone. Perhaps they were frightened away by the coming of the electric light, as were the goblins, who took to their heels the instant the clicking of switches banished the darkness of their lairs. Or do ghosts have substance only in the eye of the beholder, conjured there by the tuning-in of a receptive mind to the thoughts of some long-dead person who, standing on the identical spot, had seen what later appeared as spectres in living flesh and blood? I do not know why the ghosts have vanished, nor the reason why—when I was a child—they were so real to me, but I was sad to hear of their passing, for they were my friends.

Acknowledgement

Part of this book appeared originally in *The New Yorker*

From a late 18th-century oil painting

WHEN I was a little girl, the ghosts were more real to me than the people. The people were despotic and changeable, governing my world with a confusing and alarming inconstancy. The ghosts, on the other hand, could be relied on to go about their haunting in a calm and orderly manner. Bearded or bewigged, clad in satin or velvet or nunlike drapery, they whispered their way along the dark corridors of the castle where I was born and spent the first ten years of my life, rarely interfering with or intruding on the lives of the living.

My mother couldn't understand why the servants were frightened of the ghosts. Sitting in the sunny bow window of the Big Drawing Room, she would watch yet another maid — scanty possessions stuffed into a carpet-bag — fleeing down the drive that led through towering beech trees to the main road, and sigh plaintively. "I can never get them to understand that the ghosts won't *hurt* them," she told us. "If only they'd just ask the poor things what they *want*." And she would sigh, and bend her head again over her petit point. She was working on a set of covers for the dining-room chairs, a Sisyphean task, for even if she had completed the full set of twenty-four — which she never succeeded in doing — by the time the last was done the first cover would have worn out, and she would have been compelled to start all over again.

Her concentration on her needlework was probably not helped by the fact that she had six ebullient children — known, in pairs, as the Girls, the Boys, and the Children. I was the younger Child, the last of her family. The Boys were sent to school in England when they were about eight, and the Girls when they were thirteen, so during most of my childhood they were home only during long school holidays — four weeks in the winter, three weeks at spring, eight weeks in the summer. But we Children — myself and a sister three years older — were, during all our years in the castle, too young to be sent away to school. Whether it was termtime or holidays, we lived in the castle and it was dinned into us that if we found ourselves face to face with a ghost we must ask it what it wanted. "They only haunt because they're worried, poor things," my mother would explain in her soft voice. "Ask them if there is anything you can *do* for them. And for goodness' sake don't be frightened. After all, they're all your ancestors — whatever is there to be frightened of?"

So, as a child, I was never scared of the ghosts. But I didn't go out of my way to meet them, either. I respected their privacy, and they mine.

There were four chief ghosts in the castle. The quietest was an old man in a velvet coat, who used to sit reading in the library; he was so peaceful that one could be in the room for several minutes without even noticing that he was there, but as soon as one did notice he would softly vanish, fading into the leather upholstery. The woman in a long grey dress was just as untroublesome; her face half covered with a sort of bandage similar to that worn by some orders of nuns, she would come through the wall-cupboard of the nursery and bend over the babies in their cradles, like a nurse checking to see if her charges were sleeping peacefully. Equally unobtrusive was the woman who regularly crossed one of the upper rooms of the tower and vanished into a loft; her only fault was that she did not know that since her time the room had been converted into a bathroom, and her sudden appearance sometimes unnerved male guests who, surprised in the bath, were almost relieved to discover that the woman who had entered

2

was only a spectre. Far from quiet, however, was the red-haired young man on the stairs. He was a ghost who loved parties, and he could be relied on to turn up whenever there was festivity. Ceremonial evening dress for men having changed hardly at all for at least a hundred years, his appearance — in kilt, sporran trimmed with ermine-tails, lace-edged shirt and silver-buttoned jacket, excited no particular comment among the merrymakers. It was only when some elderly woman guest would petulantly ask my mother to tell "the young man with the red beard" not to push past people on the stairs that my mother would know he was out again. But anyone who slept in the tower could hear him on non-party nights as well, laughing and joking with his friends as he ran lightly up and down the steep spiral stairs. Often, after I was promoted from the nursery to a room in the tower, I would lie awake in the dark, with the blankets pulled high under my chin, listening to the ghosts. But I never could make out what it was that they said.

* * *

The castle stood in the middle of my father's estate, in the Highlands of Scotland. It had been built in 1210 as guard-house to a nearby monastery. Of the monastery itself only the granite gates remained, but the church that belonged to it — its first use recorded in 1078 — still served as the village kirk, and in one of the safes of the castle lay a reliquary, one of the best pieces of Celtic craftsmanship in Scotland. Believed to have once held some bones of Saint Columba, who brought Christianity to Scotland in the sixth century, it was a small house-shaped box, carved from a solid piece of wood covered in bronze and silver plates carved with intertwined animals. It was decorated with bronze medallions, their borders covered with red glaze; of its enamelled hinges, pierced to take a carrying-strap, only one remained. I

3

was unaware that it had been made more than twelve hundred years before I was born, but when I showed it to visitors I would raise the roof-shaped lid apprehensively, its strange aura making me half fear and half hope that the sanctified bones, which had long since disappeared, might have come back to rest again in the dark interior.

The castle originally consisted of a four-storey granite keep, connected by a curtain wall to a small guard tower. Probably there had been another wall that matched the first and created a courtyard containing an outside well, but no trace of this remained, although a water diviner located both hidden water and traces of precious metals in the place where this courtyard would have been, giving substance to a legend that centuries ago, in a time of attack, the inhabitants had thrown their treasures down a well.

In the seven hundred and ten years that had passed between the building of the tower and my birth, two more storeys had been added, but few alterations had been made to its basic structure. The curtain wall had been replaced by a wing of rooms, and over the centuries other wings had been

4

constructed. They radiated from the central tower like the arms of an octopus, creating an architectural fantasy, for not only was the style of each wing separated from the style of its neighbour by several generations but some of the additions had been built on different levels, turning the interior into a maze in which only a Minotaur, or a child who had been brought up there, could feel really at home.

An eighteenth-century ancestor had recorded that by 1712 the castle 'had battlements and six different roofs of various heights and directions, confusedly and inconveniently combined', and by the time I was born it had grown even more labyrinthine. Rooms led off other rooms, passages twisted, stairs spiralled dizzily and then — just when one thought one must nearly have reached the roof — changed direction and, dropping almost vertically, led back almost to the point from which one had started. There were rooms with high ceilings and rooms with low ones, narrow rooms, square rooms, curved rooms. Some of the largest rooms had right next to them rooms so small that one could, by stretching out one's arms, touch opposite walls.

My mother loved the little rooms. She had one fitted out as a miniature library, to house her treasured personal collection of books. Born and brought up in the more urbane county of Perthshire, some hundred miles to the south, she had accepted my father's proposal of marriage after a candle-lit courtship — not having seen him in daylight before agreeing to become his wife — and seemed never to have quite got over her surprise at finding herself the chatelaine of so comparatively uncivilised a place as the castle. Perhaps it was a sense of isolation from the sheltered world of her girlhood that made her look on her library as a sort of refuge; the tiny room, lit only by the vertical shafts of light that prised their way in through the arrow-slit windows, smelled of leather bindings and of the lily-of-the-valley scent she always wore.

The almost tangible presence of the characters in the books gave the room an expectant sort of magic, like the atmosphere in an empty theatre that will soon be filled with all the bustle of a play.

The front door of the castle was so heavy that a child could only just open it. Entering, one found oneself in the front hall, which had been made some three hundred years previously, when the curtain wall was replaced by the wing. It was a dark, depressing room, panelled with polished oak and hung with the stuffed heads of stags and of a Canadian wapiti that had once lived in the grounds. The seldom-used fireplace was flanked with carved angels, the supporters of our family coat of arms; they were roughly the size of a six-year-old child, and when I was about that age I used to hug them secretly, hoping that they might come to life and play with me, for I was often lonely. Against one wall stood a huge oak chest holding the fur-lined car rugs that were so necessary when we drove out in winter; against another stood two hinged-headed mandarins, brought back by some ancestor from a voyage to the Orient; made of papier maché so closely compacted that it felt like porcelain, they nodded inscrutably in the gloom, perpetually out of time with the ticking of the grandfather clock. Once a week, my father went from room to room, winding all the clocks in the castle. When the cord-suspended weight of the hall clock was cranked up, giving it the energy to run for a further seven days, there was space in the pedestal for a child to hide. To be actually inside the clock when it struck twelve was a particularly satisfying experience.

Off the hall to the left was the smoking room, even darker than the hall and redolent of tobacco. Men did not normally smoke in the drawing rooms; to enjoy their pipes or cigars they were banished to the smoking room or to the newer billiard room, which adjoined it. Under the silk-shaded

6

lights, the green surface of the billiard table stretched down the centre of the room. The walls were decorated with sporting trophies — animal heads from Africa, or plaster models of outsize fish. Built into one corner was a sacred stone, seven feet high and carved with a primitive cross; it dated from the ninth or early tenth century, but until the billiard room was built in 1888 had simply stood outside in a field.

Because we might damage the cloth, we children were not allowed to play billiards, but sometimes we were allowed to stay in the room when a game was in progress and would run busily round the heavy-legged table, picking the ivory balls out of the pockets; when we grew tired, we would lie on our backs beneath the table, drawing pictures on the underside of its slate bed with the green chalk kept for marking the ends of the cues.

The smoking room butted up against the guard tower. The little circular room at the foot of this tower, reached through a door so small that one almost needed to consume an Alice-in-Wonderland 'Eat Me' cake in order to pass through, was called Meg's Hole. Legend had it that Meg, married to an early owner of the castle, had been left behind while he and the other men had gone out to meet a rival clan, who were on their way to attack the castle. But the attacking clan had circumvented the defenders, and Meg, glancing out of a tiny window in the guard tower, had spied the enemy advancing up the drive. Having a pretty shrewd idea of what would happen to her if she was captured, she had grasped the shaft of a huge meat hook that hung from the ceiling of the small room, pulled herself up, and, letting go sharply, impaled herself through the throat on the barb. There the invaders found her when they entered the undefended tower, and there they left her for her husband to see when he returned home.

For a very long time after her death, the dark marks of her blood were said to have stained the stone floor under the hook, and, discovering that they had finally worn away, my brothers hastened to touch them up. After all, they reasoned, if visitors were too ignorant to tell the difference between blood and red paint, what could be the harm?

Above Meg's Hole was my mother's little library, and above this was the museum. Circular, like both the rooms below it, the museum was ringed with shelves, on which were set out all manner of curios, mostly connected with rocks or fossils or skeletons. I wasn't allowed to touch any of these, so I found the museum boring; above it, the guard tower ended in a little round dressing-room. All four floors of the guard tower were connected by a tiny, cramped, curving stone staircase.

Turning right instead of left from the hall, one entered the base of the main tower and, passing the foot of the small spiral stairs that led up to the first floor, found oneself in a low, stone-floored passage. Opening off this passage were the wine cellar, the beer cellar, the lamp room, the butler's pantry, and the silver room. They were all vault-ceilinged and very dark. At the end of the passage was one of the new wings. It had been built about the seventeenth century and contained the servants' hall, the cook's private sitting room — known, for some long-vanished reason, as the housekeeper's room — the menservants' bedrooms, and some storerooms and larders, most of the latter facing due south. Branching from this wing were three other wings; one-storeyed, they held the kitchen, the scullery, the dairy, the game larder, the two laundry rooms, and an inner and outer gun room.

The outer gun room was littered with muddy boots, wet mackintoshes, dogs' leads, discarded lunch baskets, empty ferret boxes, newly killed game, leather-seated shooting sticks, and string-sided gamebags. Rough, red-faced beaters tramped in and out — smelling, in their wet, work-soiled

8

tweeds very like the Labradors and spaniels that, just returned from a shoot, lay in exhausted, furry heaps in the dark corners. In contrast, the inner gun room, which opened off it, housed some of the family's most valuable possessions — the 12- and 20-bore sporting guns, which, in pairs, stood on their stocks in baize-lined, glass-fronted cabinets; alongside them were the rifles for killing stags, and the small 'four-tens' with which children learned to shoot. Pistols lay neatly beside boxes of ammunition. Oil, cleaning rags, ramrods, and small tools were laid precisely on the window ledges. The room smelled of oil and old gun-powder, overlaid with the faint odour of abraded steel; in atmosphere it seemed halfway between an operating theatre and a shrine.

Beyond the gun rooms stood long weatherproof boxes containing the salmon and trout rods; nearby, in an outhouse, hung the nets and the vicious, hook-ended gaffs used for landing salmon. The reels, lines, spinners, and steel-barbed fishing flies were kept in the inner gun room, where the bright feathers of the flies burned like glowworms under the mica lids of the small compartmented boxes in which they lay.

The main tower of the castle had two spiral stairs. The small one led only to the first floor; its curved walls were encrusted with swords, claymores, broadswords, dirks, daggers, rapiers, and sabres, and, like almost all spiral stairs, it curved upward in a clockwise direction, so that a defender would have the benefit of a free right-handed swing of his sword arm against a mounting attacker. The small stairs finished at the door of the Little Drawing Room. This was a cozy room lying over the front hall. One of our four pianos was here; it was a baby grand made of inlaid rosewood, with a lyre-shaped music rest. Next to it stood a black-and-gold Chinese cabinet. By standing on the gros-point seat of the piano stool, I could reach high enough to open the doors of

9

this cabinet; inside, the drawers and doors and divisions were arranged to give the appearance of an Oriental palace. There were staircases I could make my fingers walk up and down, and secret compartments I would find and then pretend to forget, so as to give myself, all over again, the joy of fresh discovery.

Double doors connected the Little with the Big Drawing Room. Half of this was old, lying over the smoking room, and half was new, having been built when the billiard room was added in 1888. The resulting double cube made the Big Drawing Room the most beautiful room in the castle. At the point where the old and the new parts met, the walls were slightly thicker; to mask these projections, very tall gilt-framed looking-glasses had been hung facing each other across the room, and if, standing to one side of one of these looking-glasses, I peeped carefully round the frame, I could see a long corridor of mirrors reflecting each other into what seemed to be infinity. From down this mysterious gallery of glass innumerable small girls gazed back at me, silent, wondering, the strands of their hair lifting in unison with my own.

The Big Drawing Room had five large windows, facing east, west and south, and a small sixth window, shaped like a cross, facing north; the large ones were all hung with embroidered Jacobean curtains. The intricate design of birds and trees that flowed from floor to ceiling was beginning to pull away from the original linen backing, and when relations came to stay they were sometimes coerced into spending wet afternoons stitching the embroidery onto new foundations of cream-coloured sateen. My mother was indignant that the original material was perishing — after all, it was only three hundred years old.

Whenever the sun shone, it flooded through the windows of the Big Drawing Room, bathing the oriental rugs, the glass-fronted china cabinets, the Louis XIV chairs, the Tudor stump-work sewing box, and the carved and gilded Spanish Madonna that stood on a pedestal beside the grand piano. The Madonna was about four feet tall, and had at one time adorned the long-demolished palace of a dimly-distant local bishop. Nobody knew exactly how she had come to Scotland; perhaps, like the dark-brown eyes of some of the local inhabitants, she was a legacy of the Armada, a few of whose ships were driven north and wrecked on the coast of Scotland after Drake defeated the Spaniards in 1588. Tradition also had it that some of the patterns we knitted into our jerseys had also been brought to Scotland by the survivors of the Armada, who had themselves inherited the designs from the Arab conquerors of Spain.

The Madonna had a wistful face; most of the portraits in the Big Drawing Room were, however, happy ones. In pale-blue satin or creamy lace, scarlet velvet or green taffeta or white muslin, their hair constrained by ribbons or flowing free, my ancestresses held court on the walls, as much a part of our living family as if they had been seated with us round the fire. Behind them in their portraits were the familiar outlines of mountains or streams that we could still see out of the windows, and their trailing hands caressed dogs that might have come from the same litter as those that we children romped with on the floor. The Madonna, together with the most beautiful of the family portraits — an Alan Ramsay painting of a woman in cream-and-blue satin — and many other family treasures had been spirited out of the castle at the end of the nineteenth century by an avaricious nephew of the then very elderly owner; it had been a classic Victorian melodrama of exchanged deed-boxes and misinterpreted wills, ending with my mother spending much of her dowry to restore the heirlooms to the castle.

If, instead of turning into the Little Drawing Room at the

11

top of the small spiral stairs, one turned right, one entered the anteroom, a compact, vault-ceilinged room that lay outside the dining room. This dining room had once been the main living room of the castle, and had a fireplace so large that half-a-dozen people could stand inside it. The open chimney soared straight up to the top of the tower; standing in the fireplace I could look clear up to the sky and imagine only too vividly the sooty life of child sweeps who, like the hero of one of my storybooks (Kingsley's *The Water Babies*) had been forced to climb such Stygian funnels. The fire that burned there in winter was so fierce that, if we wanted to make toast, we had to use toasting-forks fashioned from the antlers of deer, the curve of the horns allowing us to shelter round the corner of the fireplace while still presenting bread to the flames.

To break the draught that this blaze would otherwise have tugged across the room, my mother placed by the door a petit-point screen, embroidered by the child of one of my ancestors in the early seventeen-hundreds. The wan face of this diligent little girl gazed down from a group portrait on the wall; near her stood her brother, in whose Edinburgh house she was spied, many years later, by Robert Louis Stevenson. In his book *Catriona* Stevenson makes his hero, David Balfour, describe how his host (whom he names) introduced 'a dry old lady' who 'sat at a frame of embroidery' as his sister (also named). The screen was reputed to have been largely stitched at a particularly beautiful bend in the river, near to the castle — a spot still known by the little girl's name; could she also have been working on it far into her old age? Six feet high and nine feet wide, with a hundred and forty-four stitches in each square inch, the making of it must have been a daunting task; I was comforted that Stevenson, through the mouth of David Balfour, twice described the old lady as 'smiling'.

The dining room had been panelled in 1707 to celebrate the union of England & Scotland, and the plaster ceiling, installed at the same time, was ornamented with a design of intertwined roses and thistles. Under the plaster ceiling there was rumoured to be a second ceiling of carved and gilded rafters, and behind a section of panelling that had been set on hinges there was an aumbry, thought to have been a 'priest's hole', where a priest could hide in the event of an attack — though it was difficult to imagine how even the thinnest of priests could survive for long in so small a cupboard. Above and to the side of the aumbry could be glimpsed a part of the frescoes that lay behind the panelling. These were thought to have been commissioned by a laird of the time of Veronese, who, admiring the paintings he had seen during his travels in Italy, had brought an Italian artist back to Scotland and instructed him to decorate the bleak walls of the room with coats-of-arms and scenes reminiscent of the Field Of The Cloth Of Gold. In the south-west corner of the room, concealed by another hinged section of panelling, was a crumbling stone staircase that had once led down to a well — useful in time of siege.

Down the centre of the room ran the dark, polished dining table; fully extended, it could seat twenty-six people. It was lit at night by a row of four-branched silver candelabra and was commanded from either end by my parents' highbacked, thronelike chairs. Two circular tables stood in the window embrasures to accommodate extra guests, and three serving tables lined the wall next to the door, ready to receive the dishes as they came up from the kitchen. Unless one was lucky enough to have a seat near the fire, the dining room was, like most of the other rooms, extremely cold.

In the wing above the servants' hall and storerooms were small, private rooms. Winding away from the anteroom, a very dark passage led first to my eldest sister's bedroom, heavy with the scent of talcum powder, and then to the boudoir — the sitting room that she shared with another sister, three years younger than herself. The boudoir housed our communal treasure — a hand-wound gramophone. During the holidays, the two girls locked themselves in the boudoir for hours on end and, with an old jersey stuffed into the speaking-horn to muffle the sound, played and re-played their scanty stock of sentimental records; my father, had he heard the clarinets and crooners, would have been sure to object. Forbidden by my sisters to join them, I lay on the sheepskin rug outside the door, listening entranced to the wicked rhyming of moon with June.

My own province — the day and night nurseries — lay beyond the boudoir, shut off from the main part of the house by two green baize doors. The day nursery was a beautiful room with a large south-facing bow window, and at varying times served as the principal bedroom of the castle; the cupboard through which the tender ghost drifted to gaze at the babies was eventually converted into a doorway, leading to a new bathroom.

From the anteroom outside the dining-room the main spiral stairs of the castle began their climb to the roof, five storeys above. Mounting the stairs, one came first to the main bedroom floor. Here slept my mother, her bedroom door secured by a brass-weighted fastener that was operated from her bed by an elaborate system of pulleys. The little wheels squeaked when she pulled the cord; secretly, I suspected that small goblins worked the machinery. Next to my mother's bedroom was my father's dressing room and, close by, a room devoted entirely to cupboards. My father had a very orderly mind, and each cupboard and drawer was clearly marked with its contents, listed as they might have been in an army quartermaster's stores. "Vests, wool, thick," or "Shirts, silk, best," the neatly inscribed labels ran. On this floor and the

14

one above were the visitors' bedrooms. Green Room, Red Room, Brown Room, White Room, Tartan Room — room after room stood permanently prepared, with fresh towels beside the china washbasins, ready at any moment for the arrival of friends or relations. Tucked in between these two floors, at a different level from either of them, were the schoolroom and the governess's room; above these was the library, with massive leather-bound volumes, too heavy for a child to pull out, and movable ladders for reaching the upper shelves. During my brothers' holidays from school, they monopolised the library, for one of their hobbies was build-ing boats, and in the library they could construct their eighteen-foot clinker-built sailing dinghy, their gunning-punt, or their canvas-skinned canoes. Because none of these could go down the spiral stairs, they were, when finished, lowered out the window on the end of a rope. Sometimes the rope broke, and the work of months would be reduced to a tangle of broken staves and split canvas at the foot of the tower. If that happened, my brothers simply started again.

In the lofty-ceilinged, shelf-encircled library there was also plenty of space for their carpentry bench, stamp collec-tions, chemistry sets, air guns, catapults, and other impedimenta. On the mantelpiece, leaning up against the silver candelabras that lit their way to bed, was a board on which they nailed skinned rat-tails, for which my father paid them a penny a dozen. The castle was full of rats.

On the fifth floor were the maids' rooms; the young girls shared a dormitory, chaperoned by the head housemaid, who had a private, adjoining bedroom. Just above this floor the stair carpet stopped, revealing the granite of the treads; as one clambered up the final flight of stairs, past the lofts piled high with mysterious boxes, with cobwebbed trunks and disused furniture, one found oneself unconsciously walking on tiptoe, to avoid the clatter of heels on stone.

15

The top of the tower was flat, and was divided into two parts. Where the stairs ended, a trapdoor led to the higher part, an enclosed area a few yards square, carrying only the flagstaff. At one side, a heavy, nail-studded door opened onto a lead-covered rooftop, surrounded by iron railings. Here were the chimneys of the central tower — the big one, which plunged straight down to the dining room, and the smaller ones leading to the library, schoolroom, and other rooms in the tower. Here, too, were the mystery chimneys, from fireplaces in rooms that nobody could find. We tied a bell on the end of a rope and lowered it down these chimneys. Yard after yard of rope vanished over the edge of the chimney pot. One of us jerked the end while others ran round the rooms below, listening for the sound of the bell; it rang, muffled, in the thickness of a wall. What was there? We listened from every angle in the passages and nearby rooms, and measured the walls, Yes, there was space for a room. But where was the door? Where were the windows? We searched the outside walls, but two hundred years previously a tax had been imposed on windows, and many had been bricked up; some of these bricked-up windows were painted on the outside to look as if they were still in use, and some were not. We never found the hidden rooms.

Around the base of the main chimney were the 'prisoners' seats' — small stone projections like flat-topped gargoyles, placed about five feet apart. Between them, heavy iron rings were set into the stone. We were told that this was where prisoners had been chained, each sitting on a stone seat with his hands tied on either side to a ring, exposed to the fatal winter weather, but as the top floor of the tower had only been added in about 1700, by which time these sort of customs had presumably died out, it might be that the seats had been moved, and that the story was a handed-down memory of the use they had served at a previous, lower level.

16

Just below the rooftop railings was the elephant — a yard-high bas-relief of an animal looking like a cross between a mammoth and a sheep dog. The legend was that during the building of the tower a man had come home from abroad with a wild story of an animal that had a tail at both ends; nobody believed him, so he incorporated a carving of the animal into the tower, saying that time would prove that he was not a liar.

A considerable part of my father's twelve-thousand-acre estate could be seen from the top of the tower. It was in many ways an ideal estate, for, except that it lacked a seashore, it contained virtually every type of land and sport to be found in Scotland. Away to the north, farm lands and forests ran right to the boundary of the estate on the south flank of a volcano-shaped mountain, some seven miles distant. South and east, more farm lands — green and gold, wooded and fenced, traced with streams and dotted with the granite houses of the tenant farmers — stretched toward the sea and the harbour town twenty miles away. To the west lay the foothills of the Grampians; on that side, the boundaries were not visible even from the roof of the castle. Partridge skimmed over the oat and turnip fields of the fertile lowland farms, and fat pheasant peered from the beech woods and coverts. The forests provided timber for the sawmills and shelter for deer, black game, and capercailzie. Streams tumbled their way through the valleys, to meet in the wide salmon river that flowed past the castle walls, and in the pine forests that covered the hills between the farming land and the grouse moors lay a dark loch, the calm of its waters disturbed only by the splash of a fishing heron or the soft *plop-plop* of rising trout. In spring and summer, it was one of the prettiest places on earth, and when autumn came, baring the trees and covering mountain, forest and field with snow, its prettiness did not fade but was transformed to beauty.

My father had no time for contemplating the loveliness of his estate. He was far too busy running it. This was not made any easier by the fact that he had had absolutely no preparation for the task, being by both training and inclination a cavalry soldier. In my grandfather's time, nobody thought of teaching a boy how to manage his inheritance; if he was the eldest son, it was assumed that he would know how to act when the time came for him to succeed. I was too young to know how my father ran the estate, but where his children were concerned he was an implacable disciplinarian, dealing with us in a strictly military manner.

No matter what we were doing, if either he or my mother came into the room we had to spring up and stand to attention beside our chairs, and at meals we sat bolt upright, like puppets suspended by strings from the ceiling, afraid to

open our mouths except to put in food. "Sit up!" "Shut up!"
"Get up!" — the commands were barked at us; my father's
word was law, and to disobey him resulted in instantaneous
punishment.

Boys were beaten, with a cane that was kept in an
umbrella-stand in the hall, along with golf clubs, old polo
sticks, and the shepherd's-crook walking-stick that my father
carried when he went to highland games. I don't remember
what punishments were meted out to my elder sisters, but
possibly because I may have ranked as a sort of substitute boy
(my father, before I was born, having hoped that I would be
one, because — being the last of his line — he was anxious
to make absolutely sure of the succession) I was also occasionally beaten, although usually I was only severely smacked.
The culprit was always sent to fetch the cane. Once, when I
was sent to get it, I was crying so hard with terror that I could
not see it through my tears; I crept back to my father and
sobbed out that I could not find it. He stormed downstairs,
located it, and beat me twice — once for the misdemeanour
and once for being a coward. After that, I always managed to
find the cane, no matter how much I was crying.

My mother, who had had a very warm and loving relationship with her own father, did everything she could to stop
these physical assaults. "Don't, dearest, don't!" she would
cry, trying to hold back my father, and then, when she saw
that he was not to be restrained, she would run from the
room. Afterwards, weeping in our darkened bedrooms, we
would hear across the courtyard the sound of her playing
Chopin on the Big Drawing Room piano; this was her way of
telling us that she was thinking of us. It would never have
occurred to her to come personally to comfort us; that would
have been tantamount to undermining my father's authority.

Usually, I knew what I was being punished for — I had
broken a rule and was fairly resigned to paying the

19

price — but sometimes I was punished for a crime that I did not know was a crime, and then misery and bewilderment were added to the physical pain. Once, I was thrashed for waiting outside the dining-room door to eat the scraps that came out from a grown-up dinner party; my father saw me and, thinking I had been eavesdropping, beat me instantly, without giving me time to explain that I was there only because I was hungry. Not that I would have had the courage to tell him — I would have feared he would speak to my nanny, who was meant to feed me, and she would have punished me instead.

I was, in fact, never quite sure who was in charge of me. I feared every adult in my life with the exception of my mother, and even she, I knew, was easily overruled by my father. Anxiously I struggled to find some pattern in the rules by which I was governed, some line of conduct which, if carefully followed, would ensure at least a reasonable safety from smacks and reprimands, but I never succeeded. Whatever I did was sure to be wrong in the eyes of at least one of the grown-ups, so that the best I could do was to try to avoid annoying my father, whom I feared most of all. Nanny would send me down to the kitchen to fetch sugar for nursery tea; as soon as I opened the kitchen door, Cook would tell me to go away, and then for half an hour I would wander up and down the long corridors that separated nursery from kitchen, trying to decide what to do. Perhaps I could pilfer some from the canisters in the pantry, but if the butler caught me he would be sure to reprimand me; Cook might get really angry if I dared go back to the kitchen; Nanny would stand me in the corner if I returned sugarless. I stood in the darkening corridor, tears dripping into the empty sugar bowl.

The question of manners was also confusing, for governesses often had different rules from parents. At breakfast, a governess might deprive me of brown sugar on my porridge — sugar being a luxury, for salt, put in during the cooking, was the more normal flavouring — because, while waiting to be served, I had not placed my hands neatly on the table, one on each side of my plate; at luncheon, my father would send me out of the room precisely because I *had* put my hands on the table — he thought they should be clasped in my lap.

So large was the castle, and so varied the occupations of its inhabitants, that often one person was unaware of what had been said or done by another. It was frequently impossible for me to know exactly what I was meant to do. If I wandered into the library my brothers, busy with their boat-building, would tell me to go and play with my big sisters, but they, when I edged diffidently into the boudoir, would break off their fascinating boarding-school conversation, stare at me coldly — and order me to go back to the boys. Mother would reprimand me for wearing unpolished shoes, but when I went to change them a maid would refuse to give me another pair because the hall-boy, slamming the door of the boot-room behind him as he ran to his next task, had flatly refused to polish any more. The lines of communication were confusingly tangled; I felt perpetually puzzled and unsure.

So, no doubt, did the hall-boy, who lived in awe of the butler. The butler was the most senior of all the indoor servants, and was in charge of the dining-room, the wine and the silver, although my father always retained the keys of the wine cellar and of the walk-in strong-room which housed the spare silver. As well as the hall-boy, the butler had a footman to help him. All our footmen were called John, irrespective of what name the parson had bestowed on them at baptism. My father announced firmly that he couldn't be bothered to learn a new name every time the footman changed, and for the same reason the hall-boy who, as well as cleaning shoes and carrying wood, cleaned the steel knives in a machine like a small hurdy-gurdy and was virtually the butler's personal slave, was always called George.

Another of George's jobs was to refill and trim the oil lamps with which the castle was lit. Every morning he scurried round the castle, collecting the lamps from drawing rooms and bedrooms and bathrooms and passages and halls and bearing them to his den below stairs where, in semi-darkness, he polished and refilled them for the evening. As dusk fell the lamps, already lit, would be borne back into the principal rooms by the butler and footman, walking one behind the other. In lesser rooms, such as the schoolroom, we lit our own lamps.

The butler and footman also waited on us at meals, handing round the food, while the hall-boy reeled to and from the kitchen, carrying a heavy mahogany tray piled high with plates and dishes.

Next to the butler in authority came the cook. She ruled the stone-flagged, raftered kitchen like the captain of an old-time sailing-ship, giving orders to her second-in-command, the kitchen-maid, and to the luckless scullery-maid, who, isolated in the dungeonlike scullery that opened off the kitchen, spent her days — and often her nights as well — scrubbing an endless cascade of dishes and greasy pots. The cook never washed so much as a spoon; she stood at the huge pine table — so frequently scrubbed that its surface resembled a wind-eroded desert — conjuring butter and flour into pastry of a cloud-like lightness, or, the butterfly back bow of her white apron turned to the room, stood at the black coal stove whisking Sauce Mousseline or Crème Brûlée with a tiny sheaf of bleached birch twigs.

"If you don't brace up, my girl, it's back to the bothy with you!" she would threaten the kitchen maid, if the willing girl was a moment late in handing her some needed utensil or ingredient. The bothy was the house where the unmarried farm labourers lived; it was run by the kitchen maid's mother, and the girl well knew that if she was sent back she would have to work even harder than she did in what the servants called 'the mansion house'. She ran from side to side of the huge, stone-floored kitchen, trying desperately to anticipate the cook's wishes.

Upstairs, the head housemaid, her white apron so stiff with starch that I could hear it rustle down the long corridors moments before I was aware of the sound of her footsteps, chivvied the second-housemaid and the under-housemaid. The under-housemaid, until she worked her way up to the rank of second-housemaid, came rather low in the servant hierarchy, and successive under-housemaids were sometimes more or less indistinguishable one from another. Indeed, when one was dismissed — they hardly ever left of their own accord, for jobs were not easy to find in the Highlands — the girl who was to be her replacement was often chosen by size. If a girl fitted the uniform of the one who had left, she got the job. Sometimes a girl of the wrong size would be taken on by virtue of being the niece or protégée of another servant, and then until she found time to alter her dress she would shuffle disconsolately round the castle, swamped in a garment three or four sizes too big for her, or, alternatively, with a precociously-developed bosom bursting out of a dress originally bought for a flat-chested schoolgirl.

The housemaids' work was hard. They swept and dusted the main rooms before the family came down to breakfast at nine, and during this early-morning work they had to fit in the job of waking every member of the family — and any guests who might be staying — with early-morning tea. They carried a brass can of hot water up to each washbasin, and in the winter lit fires in the bedrooms to drive away the frost before people got out of bed, for from November to March the cold in the bedrooms was so biting that it would

23

freeze a jug of water solid overnight — no matter what the weather, we always slept with the windows open. They laid out the clothes of anyone who did not have a personal maid, gave a brief, usually depressing report on the weather, and hurried off to have their own breakfast before starting on the backbreaking task of cleaning the rest of the castle.

As there was no electricity, all the sweeping was done with brooms. Even when damp tea-leaves were scattered over the carpets to absorb the rising dust, this was an inefficient method, and every spring carpets that were small enough to be carried out-of-doors and, suspended on poles slung beneath a particularly large old tree-branch, were beaten by male estate-workers. Eiderdowns were also beaten, escaping feathers — flying upwards for perhaps the first time in fifty years — spiralling joyfully away in the fresh spring breezes. The workers, doggedly belabouring Axminster and Wilton with wicker bats shaped like tennis-racquets, paid scant attention to the fact that the massive branch above their heads had more than once served as a gallows.

Such floors of the castle as were not carpeted had to be scrubbed or polished. Up and down the stairs hastened the maids, bearing buckets and mops and brooms; they staggered down the stone passages, lugging unwieldy pails of soapy water or, their arms piled so high with linen that they could barely see over the top, struggled between bedroom and linen-room and laundry.

The laundry occupied two large rooms off the kitchen yard. There was a washroom and an ironing room, both commanded by a genial, red-armed widow who lived, as did all the employees who were not actually resident in the castle, in a cottage on the estate. One never had a very clear idea of what either she or her two minions looked like, so thickly were they enveloped in the steam from the coppers in which they boiled the clothes. Halfway through the week, the three

24

of them moved from the washroom to the ironing room, where they thumped about with enormous flatirons that were heated on a black iron stove. Although their work was perhaps the hardest of all, they at least had the advantage that, living out, they finished at a definite hour each evening, whereas the housemaids were scurrying around hanging up clothes, turning down beds, and putting in stone hot-water bottles — known as 'pigs' — until late into the night. My mother told me that *her* mother had felt that she was being magnanimous when she had decided that her personal maid need no longer wait up each night to help her undress; previously, the girl had remained on duty until my grandmother was actually in bed, which might mean that on the night of a party she did not finish work until the small hours of the morning. We took gleeful pleasure in teasing the housemaids, pursuing them up and down the corridors on toy bicycles or pedal cars, or — using trays as toboggans — hurtling past them unexpectedly on the steep uncarpeted back stairs.

On leaving the nursery, each pair of children was allocated a maid. My brothers used to bully their maid, so they were usually assigned an old, strong-minded one, but my sisters and I had young maids, and although they always treated us with a certain deference we became real friends; the senior servants, on the other hand, dominated them unmercifully.

My father, with the greatest naturalness, dominated absolutely everyone. During meals, from his big chair at the end of the long table, he would talk to visitors or to my mother at the far end of the table. None of us children spoke unless we were spoken to first, and when our father broke off his grown-up conversations to question us about what we had been doing, we were careful to tell him only of the activities of which we were sure he would approve — fishing, shooting, riding, and so on — for if he thought we were occupied

25

in anything he considered idle, like sitting indoors reading on a fine day, he would press-gang us into some activity that he felt was more constructive, such as gathering wood or picking up stones.

Although himself surprisingly well-read, my father thought that the actual act of reading should be confined to hours when nothing more obviously useful could be done; he himself rose at six on pitch-dark winter mornings, to study old family papers in the ice-cold library; he pored over hundred-year-old bundles of letters, marking the tape-tied packets 'READ', but unfortunately never noting down any summary of the facts that he must have so diligently gleaned. Equally, he felt that any outdoor activity should, if possible, produce more than one result; when walking round the estate, for instance, he always carried a stick shaped like a golf-club, with a sharp blade where the club-head would normally be. His mind might have dwelt on some problem of estate management but simultaneously his arm swung the stick from side to side, cutting down thistles; a stick almost identical to the one he used is depicted in a fourteenth-century manuscript — St. Mary's Psalter, one of the Treasures of the British Library.

We were not allowed to think that the circumstances of our birth gave us any right to either money or leisure. Privilege, in my father's opinion, brought with it no rights, only duties, and although he did not allow us to play with the children of his tenants, he was determined that we should not grow up to consider ourselves in any way superior to them. Whatever the tenants through economic necessity made their children do, we were required to do for the sake of our characters. Because the village children had to gather wood for their mothers' kitchens, we had to do the same for our schoolroom fire, even though our own mother rarely even stooped down to put a log on a fire herself but rang for a servant to do it for her. In winter, therefore, much of our playtime was spent searching the forests for fallen branches. The equivalent work in summer was stone picking. Armed with round wicker baskets, we scoured the rocky upland pastures, carrying stones to the edges of the fields and adding them to the rough walls that separated one field from the next. It seemed in those long, hot summer days as if some devil lurked under the wiry grass, pushing up another stone to replace each one that we laboriously carried to the side of the field. Far below, the river wound through the beech trees of the valley, beckoning us with a promise of deep, cool pools — smooth-pebbled, salmon-haunted. But it was useless to dream of swimming; none of us would dare to stop work without our father's permission.

Mealtimes held another ever-present fear — that of not getting enough to eat. At the Home Farm — the one that existed for the sole purpose of supplying the castle with produce — the fat cows lowed in their stalls, letting down steady streams of rich, creamy milk, while in the five-acre kitchen garden, the gardeners laboured over regimented lines of peas and beans, lettuces and cucumbers and asparagus, cabbages and spinach. Raspberries and strawberries and plums and damsons and cherries and grapes poured into the house every summer morning, carried shoulder-high by barefoot garden boys, while in the shooting season the gamekeepers, their tweed breeches stained by the blood of their victims, impaled on the sharp hooks of the game larder the delicately-muscled legs of deer and hare, and hung, on nails hammered into the rafters, great clusters of pheasant, partridge, snipe, duck and grouse; the dead birds' heads, beaks agape, lolled sideways, the cords that circled the radiantly-feathered throats giving each plump body an undeserved air of pendulated felony. Salmon were hauled from the

27

river — struggling on the pointed steel of the gaffs — with such frequency that servants, disdaining the tender pink flesh, insisted that their contracts of service included a clause guaranteeing that salmon would not be served to them more than once a week. Towards the sea rolled the fields of oats, to be ground in autumn between the flat stones of the village mill; in winter, potatoes and turnips and carrots lay heaped in earth-covered mounds, while all the year round pigs and calves died, protesting noisily, in murky farm-yard pens. Almost all this activity was for the purpose of feeding the people in the castle, yet we children seemed perpetually hungry. Our mother never took all six of us to the same children's party, partly because, if there were competitions, our sheer exuberance caused us to carry off an unfair share of the prizes, but also because between us we would have wolfed down all the trifles and jellies and éclairs. But it never seemed to occur to her that we might have welcomed more food at home.

At luncheon in the dining room, the hall-boy would carry in a tray of heavy silver dishes, and the butler and footman, one behind the other, would advance on the table. As the first dish was handed to my mother, six anxious pairs of eyes would assess the quantity that it held. Nine small rissoles of leftover meat. Well, at least that was fair — one each (our governess ate lunch with us). Then came the potatoes — misery, there were only sixteen. Which of us would get two, and which only one? My mother took a single potato — oh, good. But then my father took four, and gloom descended on those children who were waiting to be served after him. Even the quantity of green peas was avidly estimated, and though we would never have dared to complain while actually at table, the post mortems that took place after meals were acrimonious.

"You took two spoonfuls of peas — I saw you!"

"I didn't."

"You *did*."

"Well, perhaps I *did* have a very small second spoonful, but some of my first spoonful were maggoty."

"Greedy pig."

"I'm *not*."

"You *are*."

And everyone would fall on the floor, fighting.

My parents, who had our welfare very much at heart, cannot have intended us to go hungry, but my mother's upbringing had been very religious and had instilled into her a firm conviction that it was sinful to pay attention to such worldly things as food. She had been taught that a true Christian ate what was put in front of him and thanked God for it both before and after the meal; to question the taste of what one ate — or, worse, to be interested in the quantity — was almost as wicked as studying one's own face in the glass to try to find out whether or not one was pretty. As for my father, he thought that to be greedy showed weakness of character — something not to be tolerated either in oneself or in one's children.

At our table, food was never wasted. "Eat up, child," my father commanded if one of us should leave a bit of gristle or fat. (He hardly ever addressed us by name, and when he did he as often as not used the wrong one.) Mournfully, the culprit would force the unappetising morsel into his mouth; if my father suspected that it was not actually swallowed but simply parked behind a tooth to be spat out later, he would order the child to open his mouth for inspection.

What we lacked at luncheon or dinner, though, we made up at the more informal meals of breakfast and tea. Dining room breakfast began with porridge, liberally doused with cream; after the porridge, one could take one's pick of eggs, bacon, finnan haddie, grilled kidneys, sausages or kedgeree, served from lidded silver dishes warmed by heating lamps, and finish with baps or toast or oatcakes, spread thickly with butter and home-made marmalade. Tea was equally lavish. Although between the six of us we were only allowed one cake a week — this vanishing, down to the last crumb, within minutes of being put on the table — there was always an ample supply of freshly-baked scones and drop-scones, of sticky treacly bread and large biscuits known, because of the raisins and sultanas they contained, as 'squashed flies'. Both at breakfast and tea — except for my mother and the governess — everyone, including my father, drank milk.

But we had to have reached schoolroom age before we ate in the dining room; as small children, we led almost completely separate lives from the grown-ups. For all that we saw of our parents, they might have lived in a different house. Up to the age of about six, our lives were centred on the nursery, or, to be accurate, the nursery wing, for our nanny's domain extended to the point where the heavy green baize doors shut off the wing from the rest of the house, forming a barrier that prevented our parents, leading their grown-up lives in the main part of the castle, from being troubled by the screams of their children.

Screams there were in plenty. We screamed when we were buttoned into our newly-washed liberty bodices; these were heavy cotton jackets worn next to the skin, as stiff as sailcloth and always, on purpose, one size too small, the idea being that it was good for our chests to be 'supported'. Their freshly-starched edges cut sharply into our tender skin, and the bones that ran down the front and back compressed our ribs unbearably. After a few days, the starch softened and we dressed in comparative comfort until it was time for clean underclothes, when the screams would begin again.

We screamed when nanny smacked us, and, when nanny was out of the room, when the nursery-maid smacked us as well. In theory, only nanny was allowed to administer corporal punishment, but in practice the nursery-maid only waited till she was out of earshot to get rid of her own pent-up irritation by slapping any child within reach. Perhaps the nursery-maids smacked us as often to work off the feelings of resentment that they had against the nannies as for any real naughtiness on our part. Nursery-maids, on whom a nanny would pile as much of her own work as possible, did not have an easy life.

Not all our nannies smacked us. My first nanny was kind to me, and I loved her very much. She had gone to work for my grandmother when she was fourteen and my mother was a year or two younger. From under-housemaid she had worked her way up to ladies' maid, in which capacity she had gone with my mother on her marriage. She married one of the footmen, and later, when he died, she trained as a midwife, returning to our family when children were being born and often prolonging her visits so that they lasted several years. She wore a starched cotton uniform, on which it was pleasing to rub one's finger-tips; I toddled behind her as she bustled about the nursery, patting her ample posterior with a dawning tactile delight.

"Now stop it, you rascal — you'll wear my nice dress all out!" And she picked me up and cuddled me, before putting me in my high chair with a silver thimble on the wooden tray to keep me diverted. The sunshine sparkled on the tiny facets of the thimble; outside the open nursery window starlings and sparrows chirped in the ivy. I was happy.

This nanny was an expert at spelling-talk — the art of communicating information not suitable for infant ears by spelling words at speed to another adult, and my eagerness to understand the gossip that passed between her and her cronies awakened in me my first realisation that there was a connection between the alphabet — which I had up to then

31

seen only as a collection of coloured wooden blocks — and potentially interesting words. But she left us when I was still very young, & was followed by a succession of less kindly nannies. All nannies were, of course, known simply as 'Nanny'.

On the nursery side of the green doors, Nanny's authority was total. Even the footman, carrying up fresh logs for the fire on the hall-boy's afternoon off, was berated if he dared drop so much as a sliver of bark on the patterned Turkish carpet of the nursery passage; the butler, with great good sense, never came into the nursery wing at all, choosing to preserve his dignity rather than risk a battle of wills with Nanny. Occasionally, a nanny was friendly with a cook, but more often a blood feud raged between nursery and kitchen. Nanny would complain to my mother about the nastiness of the food, and Cook, spoken to by my mother, would get her own back on the nursery by sending up a dish that was even nastier.

The day started early in the nursery wing. Through the bars of my drop-sided cot, which, as the youngest child, I occupied long after the normal age, I would watch Nanny dressing. Winter and summer, she wore a long-sleeved wool nightdress, and it was a perpetual wonder to me how she managed to dress inside it. First, she would extricate her arms from the sleeves, then a hand would come out from under the hem and lift her wool combinations off the bedside chair. Stays followed, and then a curious band of cotton known as a bust bodice. Black wool stockings, bloomers — everything was ingested by the nightdress, and then, suddenly, off it would come, revealing Nanny almost fully clothed.

Breakfast, which, like the other nursery meals, was carried up from the kitchen by the nursery-maid, was followed by playtime. We had few toys, but those we did have were substantial. In one corner of the nursery, there was a large playhouse of the kind normally erected out of doors, a pile of battered wooden bricks, toy soldiers inherited from my brothers, and sundry rag animals.

Lunch was early, and after it my sister and I would be taken for a walk. Walks with Nanny consisted of a decorous procession down one or another of the drives. Mile-long, lugubrious, these radiated from the castle like the spokes of a wheel; they were lined with huge old beech trees that in winter dripped water and in summer kept off the sun. Walks with the nursery-maid, though more amusing, were rather frightening, for it was important to her to keep us anchored in one place while she slipped away and flirted with the farm workers.

"Now, you stay there — right there under the apple tree — till I get back. And if you move so much as an inch," she would threaten us, "the giant'll come and eat you."

Legend had it that, once, the mountain that overshadowed the estate had been inhabited by a giant, who came down at night and stole food from the castle kitchen. The inhabitants, understandably annoyed, put bars on the ground-floor windows; the giant, frustrated and furious, went back to the mountain and threw stones at the castle. Although obviously a powerful stone thrower, at seven miles' range his aim was luckily not accurate; the biggest stone fell short and landed in the river, where it still lay — a boulder the size of a car, by which we judged the level of the water during floods. The mountain had the unmistakable shape of a volcano — could the legend have been a folk-memory of some distant, prehistoric eruption? Whatever the origins of the legend, the bars remained on the windows; I was small enough to slip between them, which persuaded me that a giant's hands were bigger than my entire body.

Waiting for the nursery-maid, we lay flat on our faces

under the tree, whiling away the time by studying the activities of the tiny insects that lived in the grass. Minute green creatures waved antennae thinner than gossamer-threads at other minute creatures; bugs hardly larger than pinheads scaled, with infinite precaution, Matterhorn-pebbles no higher than a breadcrumb. Centipedes hastened past, legs moving in agitated undulations; tiny red spiders pounced, like octopodian tigers from another, microscopic, world, on prey so infinitesimal that it was impossible to see whether it crawled or flew. The grass, seen through eyes at daisy-level, was as busy as a market-square. But even as we watched, we listened apprehensively for the footsteps of the giant; we knew exactly what they would sound like — heavy, earth-shaking — and there would, we were convinced, be no escaping the grasp of his vast, horny hands. It always seemed an eternity before the nursery-maid returned, her cheeks flushed, the bib of her starched apron creased and faintly smudged with grime.

After tea, we were sent to the drawing room to spend a formal hour with our parents — or, rather, with our mother, because our father was usually still out, or else busy at his desk. In summer, I wore a muslin dress, hand-smocked from neck to waist and tied at the back with a butterfly bow of ribbon; in winter, the dress was velvet, with puff sleeves, worn under a white rabbit-fur coat. The coat was necessary because of the intense cold in the corridors; it was put on before I left the nursery and taken off by Nanny just outside the drawing room door.

My mother sat at the far end of the Big Drawing Room, beside one of the two fires that, in winter, were needed to keep it at a habitable temperature. Almost always, she had visitors with her; the castle was so isolated that friends or relations who came to stay frequently remained for several weeks, sometimes even months, becoming absorbed into the daily life of the family.

The end of the room where my mother sat was brightly lit, but down by the door at which we entered it was dark. As we emerged from the gloom into the light of the oil lamps, the women would look up from their embroidery, and murmurs of "Oh, how sweet!" or "The little dears!" — quickly spoken and even more quickly silenced — would drift towards us. It was not done to praise children to their faces; girls should grow up to think that they were ugly and could be saved from spinsterhood and its attendant miseries only by sheer goodness of character; boys should be taught that they were both stupid and inherently wicked, and that only incessant displays of physical courage and unquestioning obedience to their elders would prevent their ending up in prison or — almost worse — in the colonies.

During the hour spent in the drawing room, the grown-ups played with us, but it was an artificial sort of diversion, a one-sided game played by rules we did not fully understand. A small porcelain tea set was produced, and make-believe cups of tea were drunk with much smacking of lips and cries (from the grown-ups) of "How delicious!" and "Do give me some more!" Dolls that were kept in the drawing room — small, hard-faced, with cold, uncuddly china limbs — were dressed and undressed, their tiny shoes forced onto their feet and their feathered hats tilted becomingly over their eyes. Picture books were brought out, and the pages turned. "Look! What's this, darling?"

I wasn't her darling, I longed to shout at the powdered, smiling face of the visitor — I wasn't anybody's darling, so far as I knew. And as for the animal in the picture, it was a sheep. Did she really think I didn't know a sheep when I saw one?

On one mantelpiece stood a bronze clock shaped like a drum. It was supported by a bronze cherub, poised as if to strike the face of the clock with a bronze drumstick. When the big hand and the little hand were straight up and down, Nanny would come and fetch us, to put us to bed. Some evenings, the hands seemed to move with an almost unbearable lethargy.

The term before I was six, I graduated from the nursery to the schoolroom in the tower; my sister had already been there for two years. Deliberately, my mother always chose rather stupid governesses, her theory being that only unintelligent women would understand how hard it was to learn; unfortunately, this meant that their teaching was usually very dull. We did our lessons seated at a circular table; my legs, which were too short to reach either the floor or the central pedestal of the table, prickled with pins-and-needles.

"Stop fidgeting," our governess ordered. I tried leaning my elbows on the red wool tablecloth, to ease the pressure behind my knees.

"Elbows off the table!" the governess snapped.

I tried grasping the sides of my chair seat with my hands and levering myself a few inches off the cushion.

"Whatever are you doing, child? Get on with your writing, please."

Wearily, with inky fingers, I picked up the wooden pen. It was no use. One just couldn't win.

Our governess, who had taught the four elder children before taking on my nearest sister and me, was, like my father, a strict disciplinarian. She was also extremely ugly, having been chosen by my mother in preference to several other more prepossessing candidates not in spite of, but because of, her complete lack of physical allure. Not that my father was given to seducing nubile governesses — but my mother, perhaps with a certain amount of sense, was unwilling to take any chances. When this positive gorgon of a woman — over six feet tall, flat-chested, bristly-haired, and with enormous feet — applied for the job, my mother, quickly tearing up the other applications from twenty-year-old charmers, engaged her on the spot. But for all her severity and lack of grace we loved this governess dearly, and my father, appreciating her worth and probably also seeing through my mother's gentle ruse, affectionately nicknamed her Rosy Rapture.

Incongruously, she had a passion for birds. She seemed to know every bird on the estate — lark and swallow, wren, chaffinch, thrush, blackbird, oyster-catcher, plover, blue tit, yellowhammer, and several dozen more; she knew and could imitate their calls; she knew where they nested, and the paths of their migrations; she watched them in summer and fed them in winter, and buried them (in matchbox, cigar box, or shoe box, according to size) when she found them lying, cloudy-eyed, dead in the snow. Our tedious lessons were enlivened by the bird table that she had fixed outside the schoolroom window. There came the tits, to hang upside-down on a dripping-filled coconut-shell, and the quarrelsome robins. Sparrows fought gamely for crusts with pigeons

37

more than ten times their size, and beady-eyed starlings, seeming almost to sense their low status in the avian hierarchy, hopped quickly in and out, making off with a morsel of food before any more aristocratic bird had a chance to dispute their right of entry.

In the spring, she took us bird-nesting, not for the purpose of collecting eggs — a practice of which she strongly disapproved — but to study the construction of the nests and to watch the development of the baby birds. We mapped the woods around the castle, marking each discovered nest, and out on the fields, where the plovers laid their eggs in stone-edged hollows, we fought with her inevitably losing battles against iron harrows and heavy-footed Clydesdale horses. In the academic sense, we learnt little from her except for basic skills; in the world of birds her teaching was beyond price.

None of our governesses thought of relating our lessons to the story of our family. The history of the Napoleonic wars, for instance, would have been far more interesting if someone had pointed out to us that Napoleon had surrendered to our great-great-grandfather on our mother's side, and Shakespeare would surely not have bored us so much had we known that on our father's side we were descended from King Duncan, the victim of Macbeth. Could my mother's surprising dexterity with hammer and pliers have come down to her from her great-grandfather, who, born in 1797 with both ability and ample means, had become the first president of the Institute of Mining and Mechanical Engineers and had backed Stevenson in his development of the 'Rocket'? Or her interest in literature have grown from a childhood spent among the books left by her father's first wife (the dead mother of her older half-sisters) who was a first cousin to Elizabeth Barrett Browning? Was my father's deeply-felt interest in the estate inherited from an eighteenth-century progenitor — an acknowledged innovator in the art of land management? The castle teemed with historical records; books, pictures, furnishings and *objets d'art* of every kind could have been used to capture our imaginations, but nobody drew our attention to them and we remained totally unconscious both of them and of the ancestry that had led, through nearly a thousand years of recorded genealogy, to our own births. Instead, we struggled to learn by heart a list of the books of the Bible, traced — with a sense of suffocating boredom — maps which showed the outlines of the counties of England, or laboured over such tedious tasks as darning our woollen stockings, each of the mending-threads pains-takingly criss-crossed, so that the finished effect was of a woven patch. We also learnt real weaving, setting up the pattern of our family tartan on loaf-sized looms and fashion-ing scarves and mats from wool that we had dyed with lichen, bark or herbs. One grey lichen — crottle — growing plenti-fully on the granite walls of the fields, produced an orange dye of outstanding ugliness, tingeing much of our handwork with the hue of sun-scorched earth.

When our ornithological governess, stricken by mortal illness, suddenly left us, my mother — alarmed, perhaps, by the idea that she might have to look after her own children — broke her self-imposed rule and, cabling an agency in Paris, engaged a young French girl without a preliminary interview. Mademoiselle, who arrived a week later, turned out to be dark-haired and, in a quiet way, extremely seduc-tive, but my mother need have had no fears of her so much as exchanging glances with my father, for she had not been in the castle for more than twenty-four hours before she threw herself, both literally and figuratively, into the arms of the footman. The steep spiral stairs that ran up the full height of the tower were not easily negotiated by someone accustomed to a Neuilly bungalow; we children grasped the rope that hung almost vertically down the central pillar around which

39

the stairs pivoted and, more or less air-borne, glissaded down in giant leaps of twenty or more treads at a time. Mademoiselle, hastening after us, lost her footing and fell, with a delicate Gallic shriek, straight into the arms of John, the current footman, who luckily happened to be coming upstairs at that exact moment.

This John was a most romantic-looking young man, tall, even-featured and, like many people in Scotland, red-haired. Caught as she fell down the stairs, Mademoiselle gazed up at John's brilliant mountain-blue eyes — and fell instantaneously, hopelessly in love. John, intoxicated by his first breath of French perfume, was not slow to respond.

Who could possibly blame Mademoiselle — young, pretty, and above all, lonely? A governess, although theoretically a member of the family, was, in fact, ostracised by every group in the castle. True, she taught the children and ate lunch with them and their parents, but she dined alone in the schoolroom and never, unless she was given a definite invitation, sat in the drawing room. Servants — even the ones who fought among themselves — united in resenting every governess, who to them represented almost as much work as an extra visitor in the house, without the benefit of a visitor's accompanying tip. Even the children whom she taught seized every opportunity to elude her. In the long evenings, alone in the deserted schoolroom, she sat reading yesterday's *Times* while outside the wind soughed round the shuttered windows of the castle. It was a solitary life.

Into the virginal vacuum of the schoolroom, that blazing summer, erupted John, carroty curls springing rebelliously from restraining Brylcreem, uniform buttons agleam. He and Mademoiselle conducted much of their romance through the medium of song. Beside the schoolroom piano stood a walnut music-stand stuffed with leather-bound scores of Bach and Chopin and Beethoven and Mendelssohn, and also,

40

for the training of our young voices as well as the exercise of our fingers, a volume of Scottish songs. Musical notes fortunately being the same in all languages, it was not long before Mademoiselle was fingering her way tentatively through the air of 'Annie Laurie'.

It was when she had mastered the cadences of Maxwelton Braes and was groping her way through the opening bars of 'Coming Through the Rye' that John, hurtling in with the schoolroom tea-tray, suddenly burst into song.

Gin a body meet a body, coming through the rye,
Gin a body meet a body, need a body cry?

he carolled in a clear, strong baritone.

I gazed, open-mouthed with astonishment, but Mademoiselle, quickly rising to the occasion, dimpled prettily and, with a suddenly-developed dexterity, hastened to play the accompaniment to the next verse. John sang on, and after a while she joined in with a hesitant soprano.

In some ways, Scottish dialect is nearer to French than it is to English, and once they found that they could sing duets together, John and Mademoiselle must have felt that they had discovered an almost ideal method of overcoming the language barrier. Every evening, when he came to fetch our tea-tray, John would linger in the schoolroom. Conscious although I was that he should really not be there, I was secretly delighted, for he played Snap with me, and did fascinating conjuring tricks with glasses of water and lengths of string. He taught the schoolroom dog how to Die For The Country, and above all, he sang duets with Mademoiselle.

I lay on the bearskin hearth-rug, replete with scones and raspberry jam, watching Mademoiselle as, seated at the upright piano in her pretty foreign clothes, she tried out first one key and then another. John, an elbow propped nonchalantly against the piano's polished candle-holder, leant sol-

41

icitously over her, turning the pages of the music album. And then they would sing.

'On the bonnie, bonnie banks of Loch Lomond', 'Over the sea to Skye', 'Weel may the keel row' — the familiar verses and melodies filled the darkening schoolroom and drifted out of the narrow windows, to mingle with the whirr of the wings of a late swallow or the high, almost inaudible squeak of a hunting bat. Unnoticed beside the dark chasm of the unlit fire, I hugged the snuffling, sleeping dog, and wondered why it was I felt so happy.

My brothers, who had respected but not actually loved the previous governess, treated Mademoiselle with unaccustomed tolerance; towards either a governess or visiting child that they did not like they could, however, be merciless. We had no relations on my father's side except for a morose uncle, married incongruously to a frail, exotic American; on my mother's side, though, we were liberally supplied with uncles and aunts, whose progeny — coming from less spartan homes than ours — were ritually despised by my brothers. Small cousins, wearing modish clothes from Harrods or The White House, would be dragooned into crossing a nearby ornamental burn on a whippy, single-plank bridge; this burn, coerced at some date prior to 1782 — when it was featured in a painting — into a glassy ribbon punctuated by waterfalls, was made even more alarming by the fact that at certain times of the year it swarmed with baby eels. The same luckless cousins would be abandoned, candleless, in vaulted cellars, or lured into tree-houses, from which their pitiful wails, hours later, would signal their paralysing terror of attempting a lone descent. Any governess whom my brothers decided to hate would find a live hedgehog in her bed, or be plied with elaborately-embroidered tales of ghosts, subsequently to be awakened in the small hours by mysteriously-banging doors. Their ghostly inventiveness reached its peak

42

one dark night when, to get rid of a particularly unpopular governess, my brothers wrapped themselves in white sheets and lay down in the massive white schoolroom bath; the governess, groping for the taps by the flickering light of a candle, suddenly found the floor of the bath heaving up towards her, its macabre groans magnified horribly by the porcelain sides of the bath.

As soon as we were judged old enough to take care of ourselves, we children were turned loose out of doors when lessons ended. The daily life of the estate provided countless fascinations. Down one of the drives we might find the foresters, lopping a dangerous branch off an old beech tree; later, we would come on them felling holly or ash for the fires, or planting, on some hill too barren for even the most stalwart farmer to cultivate, a new plantation of bristly baby pines or soft, ethereal larches.

In a field near the end of one of the drives was the shepherd's caravan, surrounded by the lambing pens to which the mountain ewes were brought in springtime. Here we went to watch the sheep giving birth and to help the shepherd feed bottles of milk to orphan lambs. The shepherd's caravan, heated by an iron stove as small and as black as an opera hat, smelled of warm milk and sheep wool; along one end ran the shepherd's bed — a single wood plank only about a foot wide, covered with a grey homespun blanket. He drank the same milk as he gave to the lambs and so, whenever he offered it to us, did we, while his two brindled sheepdogs watched us from their corner by the stove, hopeful of leftover drops.

Perhaps because of its atmosphere of danger, the stone quarry held a special attraction. Here the brawny-armed quarry-men battled the cliffs of grey granite with gunpowder, pickaxe and wedge. The warning hooter would moan down the valley, followed a minute later by the smoke of the gunpowder, which, in turn, was followed by the sound of the detonation. If we were free, these signs that the quarrymen were at work sent us scampering for our ponies, so we could ride up and watch the fun. We were, of course, forbidden to go anywhere near the quarry while blasting was in progress, but this was an order that we habitually disobeyed. To crouch with some dust-covered quarryman behind a heap of protective boulders, waiting for the charge to go off, made me feel akin to the midshipmen at the Battle of Trafalgar, or to the drummer boys on the field of Waterloo, for the noise seemed to duplicate exactly the roar of a cannon. Only boys were allowed to light the fuses; I watched, frozen with delicious terror, while one of my brothers lit the end of the snakelike fuse and then, with a nonchalance that he surely could not have felt, strolled away to shelter. The explosion shook the ground and sent the black mountain crows that nested in the crevices of the rock protesting through the dust-filled air.

After the explosion, the quarrymen, skilled in detecting the faults in the grain of the granite, split it into blocks with wedges. The best blocks were shipped to London, where they

44

were used in the building of the Thames Embankment, but most of the stone from the quarry was used for cottages, farmhouses and farm buildings. The highland cottages were very solidly built. They might lack even the most primitive amenities — a cold tap was considered something of a luxury in a district where water was usually fetched from a stream or well — but their walls were of rock. Like the church in the village, they could be expected to last for anything up to a thousand years.

The small, rejected pieces of rock went to the stone breakers, who sat at the sides of the roads on short, one-legged stools. They would reach for a stone from the pile beside them, toss it a yard or so in the air to get its feel and balance, and then, holding it in the palm of one hand, strike it sharply with the small hammer that they held in the other. No matter how unyielding the stone appeared, it always broke, and they would repeat the process with the larger fragments until all were reduced to a suitable size for mending the road.

Close to the quarry on a rough patch of ground stood the permanent pens of the sheep-dip. Sheep-dipping, which was the idea of a farmer-turned-chemist from the border town of Coldstream, had only been in fashion for about a hundred years. Prior to that, anyone wishing to rid a sheep's coat of parasites had had to wash the animal by hand. Now, it was a job carried out by professionals who travelled from estate to estate, easily recognizable by the colour of their arms, which were stained right up to the shoulder by the yellow liquid into which they plunged the sheep. The black-faced mountain animals were marshalled by sheepdogs through a series of interconnecting pens, which finally led them to a sunken concrete bath filled with creamy-yellow disinfectant; in pits on either side of the bath stood the dippers — rubber-aproned, blasphemous — and as each sheep was precipitated out of the final pen they grasped it firmly, closed its nostrils

45

with their fingers, and plunged it under the liquid. The whole ceremony resembled nothing so much as a rowdy mass baptism.

Shearing, also, was done by travelling professionals. Although home spinning had almost entirely died out by the time I was born, we still used many articles that had survived from the days when, instead of being sold, the wool from the sheep was processed on the estate. This local wool was durable stuff; I slept during most of my childhood under homespun blankets embroidered '1745' — the year of Bonnie Prince Charlie's abortive rebellion against the English. My family, being at that time more practical than romantic, had fought against Bonnie Prince Charlie, a fact that had not — even nearly two hundred years later — been forgotten by our neighbours. To tease those who still felt particularly indignant, my father had been known to place them, at dinner, directly facing the portrait of our ancestor the judge, who had been the head of our family when the Prince of Orange (William III) had taken over the Stuart throne.

Perhaps the activity we loved best was riding. We could ride wherever we wished, for, although most of the farms were let to tenants, our right to go where we chose was never questioned. The only snag to riding was that from time to time my father took it into his head to teach me how to do it. Left to myself, I simply got onto the Shetland pony that was habitually tethered half-way down the front drive, pointed its head in the general direction that I wanted to take, and started off, unhampered by either saddle or bridle. But my father's cavalry training rebelled against such a ragged turnout, and if he came on me and was free he insisted on giving me lessons. Dumped unceremoniously on the back of one of the pensioned-off hunters or polo ponies kept in the stable, bare legs pinched between stirrup leather and saddle, I was sent to a paddock, down one side of which stood a line of jumps. Sweating with fear, I was made to cajole my horse into position at the start of the line, where my father stood, legs apart, flexing and unflexing a formidable, tassel-ended whip. *Crack*, the whip came down on my horse's rump. The animal leaped forward, and I grabbed the saddle pommel.

"Sit up straight! Knees in! Heels down!" yelled my father as the horse rocketed out of control over the jumps.

But it was no good. I always fell off. Alas, no fall, unless it resulted in unconsciousness or a visibly broken limb, excused me from the rest of the lesson. It never seemed to occur to my father to teach me how *not* to fall off; trial and error was his method, and because my errors were so painfully obvious the trials continued.

In contrast, the pony rides that we took on our own were filled with delight. No matter in which direction we set out, we seldom reached in an afternoon the boundary of the estate, and, as each direction had its own particular enchantment, we sometimes gave the ponies their heads and let them go where they pleased.

To the north lay the river and the dark coniferous forestry plantations. No bridge crossed the river near the castle and we would ford our ponies through the water, their unshod feet nimble on the boulder-strewn banks; climbing out, they shook their stocky, unclipped bodies, sending a rainbow of water drops arching through the sunshine. In the plantations lived the deer — not the heavy-antlered, red deer of the mountains but gentle, timid, roe deer, who fled from us, their white scuts bobbing like rabbit tails, down the fern-edged, moss-carpeted aisles of the forest.

Or we might go west, toward the foothills of the Grampians, bracken-covered, birch-decked, their flanks scored by busy, tumbling streams. Here lived all the animals that, driven from the lowlands by the advance of agriculture, were neither skilful nor tough enough to survive the more rigorous

47

life of the mountain tops. Rabbits bounded in and out of sandy burrows and fought desperate, doomed battles with predatory weasels; coots and snipe disputed possession of the secret pools; voles and water-rats tunnelled the banks of the streams, while their small relations, the field mice, hurried through the coarse grass. Only the flies, following our ponies in relentless swarms, marred the perfection of the afternoons.

South and east, fertile land dotted with farms stretched away toward the distant sea. There were about a hundred dwellings in the estate, and we knew them all. The sister next to me — the elder Child — had an especially close relationship with our father's tenants, and was welcomed wherever she went; farmers' wives, their homespun skirts covered with aprons fashioned from discarded sacks, would come to their doors as we rode by, inviting us in for milk and oatcakes. The oatcakes cooked over open farmhouse fires were infinitely more delicious than the ones we were given at home; sometimes we would arrive just when they were being made and would watch the thinly rolled mixture of coarse oats and beef dripping being placed on the black iron griddle and swung on a hook and chain over the peat fire. The smell of the crisping oatcakes mingled not unpleasantly with that of warm woollen clothing, and with the lingering steam from the latest batch of boiled potatoes, for, in many farmhouses, mid-day dinner consisted only of a big bowl of plain boiled potatoes, washed down by milk.

Sometimes, after lessons, a combination of hunger and greed drove us to raid the kitchen garden. Like most castles in Scotland, ours was surrounded by lawns, embellished by ornamental trees and banks of flowering shrubs, but it had been — as was reported by an early-nineteenth-century writer — the 'fashion to remove the fruit and vegetables to an inconvenient distance from the cook', and our main, or kitchen, garden, with its big vegetable patches — each

48

covering nearly half an acre and edged with herbaceous borders — was about a quarter of a mile away. Since it was ringed by a high granite wall and guarded by the dour head gardener, backed up by garden-boys, raiding this garden was no easy undertaking. The only door that was not overlooked was kept locked; my mother had a key, but we never thought of asking for it, so natural did it seem to us that we should be excluded.

Secretly, we made rope ladders, and prospected adjacent trees for overhanging branches. Although we were happy to scramble over the wall and grab anything that could be eaten — from peas to unripe apples — the citadel to be stormed was the grape house, where hung cosseted, steam-ripened pendants of black grapes destined for our parents' dinner parties. An attack on the grape house demanded tactical planning, the deployment of all available children, and particular courage on the part of whoever was chosen for the final assault. As the doors of the grape house were always locked, the only way of getting in was through the iron ventilation louvres, which, even when fully extended, offered a passage only about nine inches high. Usually we succeeded in capturing a bunch and getting clean away, but one awful day the head gardener caught my second brother half-way in through a louvre and, quickly winding the crank that shut it down, imprisoned him by the waist. Standing outside, he beat my brother's lower half with the handle of a garden spade, while on the other side of the glass my poor brother's upper half yelled helplessly.

If we lacked time to go riding or courage to raid the garden, we could always find something to do at the Home Farm, whose buildings formed a square contiguous to that of the garden. It offered almost endless diversions. At one end, raised above the level of the farmyard, lay the duck pond, complete with an island. Here were watered not only the

49

huge slow-moving farm horses but also the riding horses, whose stables faced the pond. Fat ducks destined for the table fished, tails up, in the shallows, and moorhens darted warily in and out of the surface-trailing branches of the willow trees that edged the shores. This was a good place to try out my brothers' homemade canoes, which had to be tested before we could risk taking them on the river; resolutely, we paddled across the dangerous waters of the Aegean or the Java Sea, to beach our craft on the reedy island, transmogrified for a single summer afternoon into Crete or Mindanao.

The duck pond also provided a reservoir of waterpower for the circular saw that cut up logs and for the threshing machine that separated the oats. There was little difference in the texture of the oats roughly ground to make our porridge and that fed to the animals, and if our next meal seemed a long time away we would sometimes climb up the steep wood ladder that led to the storeroom above the thresher and, thrusting our hands into the animals' bins, stuff our mouths with the raw grain intended for the horses.

Next to the threshing machine was the dairy, with its uncovered buckets of milk and large flat pottery bowls in which the cream rose thick to the surface, to be skimmed off by the dairy-maid and thumped into butter in a barrel-like hand-worked churn. Beyond the dairy lay the cow shed. Here in semi-darkness stood the rows of placid milk cows, munching sliced turnips as they awaited the arrival of the milkers, with their three-legged stools. In a heavily barred enclosure, the bull — ring-nosed — snorted and stamped, while, outside, the wobbly-legged calves lifted their soft, wet noses and licked our proffered hands with rough, hesitant tongues, perhaps mistaking our outstretched fingers for the udders of the mothers from whom they had been so summarily parted.

In the creosote shed, a long tank filled with the black creosote in which fence posts were soaked looked like a slit in

50

the surface of the earth, and gazing at the crocodile shapes of the half-submerged logs I was convinced that the tank was bottomless, that the viscous liquid was oozing directly from the centre of the world.

Once my elder brother, dancing cheerfully on the logs in an attempt to make them rotate under his feet, fell in, and was blinded for a week. White-faced, he lay in bed, with the curtains of his room drawn, while my father — resolutely showing no signs of perturbation — sat by the tiny crack of light that was allowed to enter, first reading him *White Fang* and then — so that the time would not be entirely wasted — selected pages of *Chambers' Encyclopaedia*.

In one corner of the farmyard, near to the creosote shed, was the carpenter's workshop. The carpenter, who did all the woodwork not only in the castle and on the Home Farm but on the other houses and farms on the estate, was dry and thin, like one of his own seasoned planks, and not given to any unnecessary talking, but as he usually had an apprentice working under him we could learn a lot simply by listening to the lessons that he gave. Perched on a trestle, we watched while he taught the mysteries of dovetailing and mitring, of planing and pinning and rebating and chamfering. Rasp saws, tenon saws, hacksaws and keyhole saws were lifted from their wooden pegs and their different uses explained and demonstrated. Round nails, oval nails, French nails, panel pins and tacks were hammered home, to show their proper functions. Evil-smelling pots of glue simmered on a paraffin stove by the half-open door, and heavy wooden vices groaned as, with a twist of an oaken bar, they were tightened around the homegrown pine planks.

On the north side of the farmyard stood the bleak and comfortless bothy, where the unmarried farm labourers lived. Stone-floored below and virtually windowless above, lacking all indoor sanitation, the only thing that could be

said for it was that it was, at least, no worse than the accommodation the men would have found on any other farm. It was ruled by a hard-working widow, who fed her ravenous charges on great mounds of boiled potatoes, basins of scalding-hot porridge, pint mugs of fresh milk, and a sort of thick broth made from onions, turnips, carrots, barley, and the carcases of rabbits. It was rough but healthy food, and must have suited the inhabitants of the bothy, for they worked and frolicked with unflagging vigour.

The bothy looked straight out onto the central midden — as large as a tennis court — where all the manure from the stables and cow-shed was dumped. My accident-prone elder brother, chased across the farmyard by a bull, was saved from a goring by running across the midden; comparatively light in weight, he raced over the straw-threaded surface, while the pursuing bull, bellowing furiously, sank up to its stomach in the steamy morass. Hens and great grey rats, bigger than the ones that gnawed and fought in the walls of the castle, lived on the midden; the hens' eggs were sent in to the castle kitchen whether they had been lifted from a clean straw nest in the barn or from beside a spatter of fresh cow dung in the farmyard. Nobody minded.

Around the corner of the cart shed, where the great wooden-wheeled farm carts squatted, their shafts pointing up, awaiting the black-harnessed, brass-decorated farm horses, was the kennel of the shooting dogs. We could hear them long before we rounded the cart shed. They bayed and barked and whined and yelped in their wire-netting enclosure, and when we neared the gate they hurled themselves against the netting in a struggling mass of legs and tails and white-fanged, vermilion-edged jaws. Fed only once a day, they ate rapaciously, wolfing down meals that were not so very different to those ladled out in the bothy, except that, in the kennels, the rabbits were boiled complete with skins. Behind the slavering dogs, the ferrets in their cages darted from side to side, their snakelike heads weaving nervously.

In spite of their ferocious appearance, the shooting dogs were well trained. They had to be, for in the life of the castle, shooting came, in theory, second only to religion. In fact, of course, it took precedence over absolutely everything.

As the summer wore on and the grain ripened in the broad meadows, the thoughts of all the male inhabitants of the castle turned inexorably to slaughter. Killing was not only their favourite pastime; it was also the activity for which they had had the most intensive training and for which their upbringing and tradition best suited them. But whereas their ancestors, feeling the blood lust rising in their veins, would snatch a claymore from the wall and set out to decimate a neighbouring clan, the men of my childhood confined their murderous intentions to the animal kingdom. Strangely, none of them seemed consciously to think of this in terms of a destruction of life; it was more a test of skill, on a par with the archery contests of previous centuries.

As soon as they were tall enough to hold a gun — which was when they were about eight years old — the boys learned to shoot, first with a four-ten, then with a 20-bore, and finally, when they were fully grown, with a man-sized 12-bore shotgun. A boy's coming-of-age present from his father might be a matched pair of Purdey or Holland & Holland guns, costing considerably more than a year's wages of a groom or keeper.

Small boys practiced for hours, intent on knocking empty cans off fence posts; my brothers went one better, using my nearest sister and me as moving targets for their air guns, which, being relatively harmless, they were allowed to use without supervision. The lawn behind the castle was planted with groups of rhododendron bushes, and we were made to run from one clump to another while our brothers took pot-shots at us. It all, they assured us — as we sprang, howling, from one bush to another — helped to improve their eye.

To have a good eye — that is, to be both quick and accurate with a gun — was a guarantee of popularity in the world of men. A young man who could be relied on to bring down any bird that flew within range was sure of many invitations to shooting parties; a host anxious to improve the sporting record of his estate was even known to invite someone he positively detested, if by so doing he would increase the quantity of the kill. That the game record, or bag, should be good was not only a matter of pride and a source of income — any game not eaten or given away was sold — but also a kind of insurance against hard times, for should lack of money force a landowner to let his shooting, the price he got for it would be in direct ratio to the amount of game that had been bagged in previous years. Except that toward the end of the season word might go out to spare the young hens to ensure an adequate breeding stock for the following spring, there was no limit to the number of birds that could be shot.

The opening of the shooting seasons varied with the type of game. By far the most important was that of the grouse

— August 12th. The preparation for this took up much of the year. As soon as the snow had melted from the grouse moors in the spring, the keepers set to work repairing the butts. These were small hides made of piled-up turf, placed in lines over the moors just over two gunshot lengths apart. The weather was watched anxiously for conditions favourable to the survival of the baby birds; a really wet spring could drown many of them soon after they came out of the egg, and exceptionally cold weather could result in death from starvation. The grouse fed on young heather shoots; if icy conditions prevented the heather from sprouting, they died. To encourage new growth in the heather, one-seventh of all the moor was burned each autumn; day after day, fires raged across the hilltops, kept from spreading into areas where they were not wanted by a small army of workers, who beat out the flames with long-handled birch brooms. If the fires seemed to be getting out of control, the men might spend several days continuously on the hills.

At the beginning of August, it was impossible to get a sleeping-berth on the night train from London to the north; every one had been booked months in advance by the friends of the grouse-moor owners, travelling to Scotland to shoot on the Twelfth. The castle was always crammed with visitors. All the spare rooms were opened up, and every leaf inserted into the dining-room table. The strong-room doors were swung open, and the extra silver was counted and cleaned and carried upstairs, where it joined the reserve sets of silver candelabras, whose many-armed splendours were being assembled and polished by the green-aproned hall-boy.

Each gun — the man who did the actual shooting — brought with him his dog and his loader and, if he had one, his wife, though women were not encouraged to appear on the moors, where their bright clothes were thought to frighten the birds. (Bright meant any colour distinguishable from mud.) Children, however, were acceptable, as they could be used along with the dogs to retrieve the shot birds. We would hang about hopefully, gauging the right moment to ask if we could join a gun in his butt; often we would not dare to ask, but would, like a supernumerary retriever, simply tag along, hoping that the gun would not notice us and send us home.

On the muddy floor of the butt lay the gun's dog, quivering and dribbling with excitement. I knelt beside it, oblivious of the sharp heather stalks that dug into my bare knees. Relaxed yet alert, a firearm resting lightly across his knees, the gun sat poised on his shooting-stick; beside him squatted his loader. While we waited, nobody moved or spoke, and in the still, upland air one could hear, mingled with the hum of the bees collecting nectar from the heather, the lowing of cattle down in the valley and the *chuff-chuff-chuff* of the single-carriage local train as it set off from the village station on its hour-long journey to the sea.

Then it began, at first so faintly that I strained forward, wondering if I had really heard it — the sound of the beaters approaching across the moor. I craned my neck to peer over the edge of the butt and was instantly shoved down by the loader's hand. But I had seen what I wanted. Along the horizon, the beaters were advancing, shouting and waving white flags. In line abreast, they closed in on the butts, and for all the movement in the narrowing strip of ground that lay between, it seemed that there was no living bird on the moor. Then suddenly it was as if the heather had exploded. Birds rose by the hundred and hurtled toward the guns, crying their raucous call that sounded so much like "Go back, go back, go back!" as they flew. Guns were fired and reloaded and fired again so quickly that their movement between the hands of loader and firer blurred — when the birds came over well, it was not uncommon for both firearms of a pair to get almost too hot to handle.

The noise was deafening. Crouched at the feet of the gun, with the cartridges exploding within inches of my head, I tried to hold my hands over my ears without letting go of the chain of the dog, who, excited beyond bearing, was threatening to forget his training and go barking out among the falling birds. The birds plummeted down from the sky, their brown bodies thumping into the heather. I cowered back under the overhanging wall of the butt, for to be struck by a falling grouse could be as painful as receiving a hard-hit tennis ball straight in the face.

As quickly as it had begun, it was over. The birds that had escaped the slaughter vanished over the other horizon, calling to each other as if to rally their ranks. The beaters reached the butts, and the dogs and children were set loose to run zigzag, quartering all the area within gun-range as they retrieved the dead birds. Then everyone moved off to the next row of butts, a mile or so distant, and the whole performance began again.

Around one o'clock, there was a break for lunch. Striding downhill, we would come on a small group of ponies, from whose panniered backs my mother and other women would be unloading a gargantuan picnic lunch. Cold game, ham, beef, chicken, hot lamb stew, pastries, baked potatoes, salads, biscuits, fruitcakes — everything was laid out on white tablecloths spread over the grass. Deer-horn drinking cups were filled and refilled with beer and cider and lemonade (except in cold weather, whisky was not provided). Discreetly separated from us by a hillock or a clump of trees, the loaders and dogs shared 'doorsteps' — jaw-stretching sandwiches several inches thick, stuffed with homemade cheese or last year's scarlet raspberry jam.

Sitting close beside their mothers, shiny-nosed, wind-blown girls — visitors to the castle for the shooting-party — gazed resentfully at other neatly-pretty girls who had spent the morning in bed, and, noting how all the young

57

men were clustering around them, bitterly regretted the misplaced enthusiasm that had led them to rise early and go out with the guns. With his head resting on a half-empty cartridge-bag, the oldest member of the party snoozed peacefully, a half-finished glass of port tilting in torpid fingers.

Duck shooting was similar to grouse driving, except that the guns stood in hides around the edge of a lake. Duck have very good hearing, and absolute silence was necessary. The dog who whined or the child who sneezed as the guns crept toward the woven-willow hides would not be taken on the next duck shoot. Then there were the pheasant shoots, and the partridge shoots, and the killing of capercailzie — those huge blackish-grey birds that haunt the higher fir forests — and of snipe and woodcock and hare. Rabbits, classed as vermin, were shot year-round, hunted out of their burrows by the ferrets that lived in the dog kennels. These ferrets, very nearly as savage as their wild cousins the weasels, could bite their way out of most containers, and were carried to the warrens in small, strong wooden boxes, which the keepers placed in the canvas-and-netting game-bags that they wore slung over their shoulders. Picked from its box by the scruff of its neck, a ferret would be pushed down a rabbit hole, and moments later a rabbit would bolt out and be sent tumbling by a blast of shot. The ferret, following the rabbit in eager, undulating leaps, was caught and returned to its box, where it would scratch and mew in frustration until lifted out for the next burrow. The more intelligent ferrets caught and devoured a rabbit underground whenever they got the chance; this was considered rather disloyal on their part. Even the gentle roe-deer were shot — not for sport but because of the damage they did to the crops. Nobody would have minded if they had simply eaten their fill of oats and turnips and gone on their way, but they trampled the grain they did not nibble and in the turnip fields wandered from row to row, taking single bites that let in the rain and ruined twenty roots for each one that they consumed.

When the men tired of killing birds and beasts, they turned their attention to fish. The wide river that flowed almost under the walls of the castle teemed with fins; one had only to dangle a line from the bank or to wade, rubber-booted, through the clear, stone-floored shallows to be almost certain of hooking a silver-scaled salmon or a wriggling brown-speckled trout. Before we were judged old enough to hold a rod, my sister and I contented ourselves with trapping minnows and sticklebacks and the mysterious Sargasso-sea elvers in the ornamental burn. Or we went to the upland loch, where a boat was kept, and we could linger in the autumn evenings, poised as if on a sheet of glass, while trout rose secretively in the dusk and the midges browsed on our unprotected hands.

The loch had an island, on which there was a ruined stone summerhouse. Underneath, steps led down to a damp and echoing cavern; before the invention of refrigerators, my ancestors had the ice of the lake cut into blocks and stored here, resurrecting it the following summer to chill their sorbets and trifles. It lacked only a genie to be Aladdin's cave;

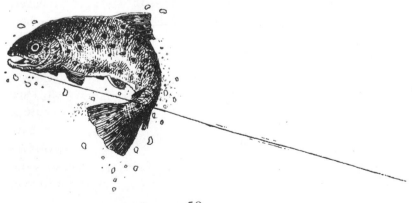

we hid a shining new penny there, confident that before our next visit it would be transformed into a bag of gold.

The abundance of game on the estate did not, of course, escape the notice of poachers, against whom the gamekeepers waged an incessant and, at times, bloody war; because the poachers were often local men and feared recognition by a vigilant gamekeeper, they wore masks — a habit that gave them an aura of sinister mystery. The most frightening of the poachers were not, however, the ones who worked by night but the pearl poachers, who operated in broad daylight. The river that ran past the castle held freshwater oysters, which produced quite large pearls. To find these oysters, one had to wade through the shallows carrying a glass-bottomed wooden box, which, when lowered slightly below the surface, allowed one to see clearly under the water. Thieving as they did for monetary gain, and not, like the game poachers, for food, the ragged pearl poachers — mostly strangers to the estate — were a menacing breed.

One bright day in late spring, my father was dressing to go to Edinburgh. Normally, for a journey so far south, he would abandon the kilt that he wore at home and put on an ordinary trouser suit, because, although Edinburgh was the capital of Scotland, to us northern highlanders it ranked as lowland, and in the lowlands we wore English clothes. We called ourselves 'Scotch' (never 'Scottish'), and we referred to men who wore kilts in Edinburgh — or, horror of horrors, outside Scotland — as 'damn Scotch'. Men who got married in London wearing highland dress were also 'damn Scotch', and so were people who (except at the Caledonian Ball in Park Lane) danced reels south of the border. Whether from politeness or a less commendable feeling of superiority, we never criticized the dress of foreigners, in which category we included the English. They could wear tartan whenever or however they liked.

But this spring morning my father was putting on not an ordinary suit but a medieval uniform of hunting green, for he was going to Edinburgh to take up his duties as an Archer. The Royal Company of Archers, a sort of part-time regiment, formed the King's personal bodyguard in Scotland, and was elected from Scotsmen who had distinguished themselves in one way or another.

The uniform consisted of trousers and a tunic of green cloth, trimmed with a black braid on crimson velvet. Round the waist was a black leather belt, the gilded buckle inscribed with the royal crest; from the belt hung a short sword of the type used by the Romans, and, next to the sword, an arrow-wiper. Nobody seemed to know whether this was to be used before the first shot, so that no particle of dust should impede the arrow's flight, or to remove blood after the arrow had been retrieved from the corpse of an enemy.

When he was dressed, my father slung a bow case, also trimmed with gilt and velvet, over his left shoulder, and on his right hip he fastened a St. Andrew's Star. Finally, he put on his head a Highland bonnet, with a white-and-green silk cockade and an eagle's feather secured with a gilded badge.

Just as he was checking his appearance in the looking glass, one of my brothers burst into the room and gasped out that there were pearl poachers in the river. My father rushed for the door, grabbing as he ran the nearest weapon to hand, which happened to be his Archer bow. We all raced to the riverbank where, sure enough, we spotted three poachers, hunched up over their glass-bottomed boxes as they moved through the shallows of the opposite bank.

"What the devil d'you think you're doing?" my father bellowed.

The poachers looked up, at first truculent and then bewildered. Accustomed to dealing with tweed-clad gamekeepers and even occasionally with kilted lairds, they

61

clearly did not know what to make of this tall, wild-looking man, dressed in green and brandishing a bow almost as tall as himself. They stared, and then turned and fled.

My father glanced downstream to assess the distance that lay between him and the moorings of the flat-bottomed boat in which he usually crossed the river, knew that if he went to get it the poachers would escape, and, not to be deprived of the pleasure of an arrest, leapt fully clothed into the river. Dogs and children plunged after him, barking and yelling. Like a pack of otter hounds we thrashed across the water, fell on the poachers, and marched them ignominiously off to the village hall, which, in an emergency such as this, did duty as a jail. Then suddenly my father realised what he had done to his uniform. The wet tunic wrinkled over him like a snakes-skin on the point of being shed, while the scarlet of the velvet trimmings was streaking the green with pink. The bow case dripped, and water-weed dangled from every one of the gilded buckles and badges. But he only laughed; proud and fierce though my father might be, he was never self-important.

The pearl poachers had been ragged, but so, too, were we children. Practically no attention was paid to what we wore during the daytime. One new set of male or female garments was bought whenever the eldest boy or girl grew out of what he or she was wearing; as there were two big boys and two big girls, this meant that the elder members of the family had, at least, the correct clothes for their sex. The boys always wore kilts and the girls either tweed or tartan skirts. But my nearest sister and I, at the tail end of the family, had to wear whatever fitted us. This was all right when the handed-down boy's garment was a kilt, but not so good when it was grey flannel trousers or striped football socks brought back from a boarding school in England. Rough hand-knitted jerseys, their snagged stitches cascading from neck to hem, were

62

gathered around our small waists by large dog collars, the brass labels of which proclaimed our names to be Rover or Thunder or Trust. When we got larger and one collar would no longer do, two collars were buckled together to make the belt. On our heads we wore ancient felt hats discarded even by my frugal father as being too shapeless to wear; they looked like wilting mushrooms and were decorated around the brims by mangled collections of fishing flies. On our feet, in winter, we wore heavy black boots made by the village shoemaker, their soles almost solid with nails; in summer, unless the weather was particularly bad, we went barefoot. During a cold summer we wore tennis shoes, but these were not replaced when our feet grew; instead, a section of the canvas was cut away to allow our toes to poke out.

In contrast, our evening dress was very formal. When we graduated from the nursery to the schoolroom, substituting for a bedtime snack of milk and biscuits a five-course dinner with our parents, we stopped wearing the short skirts of our babyhood and put on long dresses that might have come out of the family por-  traits that gazed down on us as we ate. There was one dinner dress of which I was particularly fond — a grass-green velvet, with a wide lace collar. True, it was the only one I had, and it had been worn before me by all my sisters, but I knew it to be the most beautiful thing I had ever put on. To give it variety — for I wore it almost every night for a year — I made wreaths from the troughs of hothouse flowers that stood around the Big Drawing Room, crowning myself with a different selection each even-

63

ing. Remembering how much we were discouraged from any show of vanity, I sometimes wonder how I got away with this. Perhaps nobody noticed.

My brothers, who during the day looked more untidy than the village children, came down to dinner in immaculately-pressed scarlet kilts, lace-edged shirts and velvet jackets, the silver buttons of which were embossed with our family crest. Into the tops of their tartan stockings were stuck Cairngorm-crowned skean dhus — ridge-backed knives capable not only of killing a man but of ripping him up in the process. The silver buckles on their shoes flashed when, late as usual for the meal, they swung themselves down the rope of the spiral stairs; they dashed into the anteroom just as my father was finishing his piece on the xylophone.

My father's xylophone stood in the anteroom, along with the silver-lipped letter box, into which all the family dropped their outgoing mail — unstamped, of course, for all the details of life, such as the stamping of letters and the putting of toothpaste onto toothbrushes, were attended to by servants — and the gong, which was beaten by the butler to tell guests when it was time to dress for dinner and later to announce the meal. Father had inadvertently bid for the xylophone at an auction. Finding he could not avoid paying for it, he had brought it home, and, true to his own teaching that nothing in his house should be wasted, he had learned to play. Or, rather, he had learned to thrash it with a hammer. He had no musical sense, which pained my mother, who had a good ear and considerable talent on both piano and violin. The only tunes he knew were the barrack-room songs of his army days, and they were what he played, helping his performance along by shouting the words. "Drunk last night, drunk the night before. So drunk last night, couldn't get through the door," he howled in happy abandon, out of tune, while a line of guests, be-laced, be-furred, and glittering

64

with diamonds, waited patiently to go in to dinner. My mother would pluck at his sleeve. His playing made her extremely nervous, but there was no way of persuading him to give it up. To my father, those sessions at the xylophone were bracing — the equivalent of the southern before-dinner cocktail.

Surprisingly little drinking went on in the castle, for all that it was near the whisky-distilling part of Scotland. Wine was served at dinner, and last thing at night, just before everyone went to bed, the butler brought in the silver grog tray, with its load of whisky, brandy, soda siphons, and lemonade. At this time, the men usually had a whisky-and-soda, while the women sipped lemonade. In the north, for a woman to be seen drinking whisky would have caused a minor scandal, although there were, of course, exceptions. Out shooting, if it seemed that through sheer exhaustion she might hold up the day's sport, a woman was occasionally revived with whisky-laced coffee. A woman in childbirth might also be given whisky — not if it was an easy birth but if the pains had gone on for several days and nobody could think what else to do.

Medical attention at births was not sophisticated; all the women of the estate, including my mother, were attended — if, indeed, they were attended at all — by a former veterinary surgeon. Perhaps he had taken supplementary exams and qualified as a proper doctor; perhaps he hadn't. Nobody was quite sure. Rumour had it that he had made the change from animals to people because people were easier to diagnose — they could tell him where the pain was. Because there were six of us — conveniently grouped, and with reliable keepers — he used us children like laboratory rats, to test products about which he was uncertain. Luckily for us, the drugs in his dispensary were basic and uncomplicated, so we suffered no great harm, although I did resent

65

being given the newly fashionable halibut-liver oil. "I hear this is vairy guid for the bairns," the doctor announced, holding up to the light a bottle of yellowish hue. "But I canna get any o' the village bairns tae sup it — they say it fair maks them reech. Noo, m'lady, if yon youngest one of yourn wis tae tak it, she could tell me if t'wis reely aa that bad, eh?" And he smiled grimly at my glowingly healthy face. Nobody had any idea how concentrated it was, and for the next two weeks I was given a large soupspoonful of halibut-liver oil after each meal. I howled and retched and ran despairingly around the dining-room table, pursued by my mother carrying the hated bottle. I stank of fish — my hair, my hands, my clothes — until, finally, my mother reported to the doctor that perhaps the village bairns had been right after all; it really was undrinkable. A year or two later, the same oil came out in measured drops sealed in capsules.

The doctor was one of the very few men who could get away with teasing my father, and in return he tolerated my father's libellous remarks about his medical skill. I remember him surprising my father once in the act of tying me up into a brown-paper parcel, to find out if it would — in theory, at least — be cheaper to send children to London by train or post. The doctor watched with interest while my arms and legs were secured with string. This part was easy, for, convinced that my father really intended to post me, I was paralysed with fright; but the next stage, when my father had to fit a square piece of paper around a more or less circular child, was more difficult.

"Hoo aboot sendin' ane or twa tae the orphanage, if you're that determined tae thraw them oot?" the doctor said, putting a helpful thumb on a knot that my father was struggling to tie.

"Good heaven, man, they'd be better off in a byre," my father retorted with spirit. He took a keen interest in the

66

welfare of the local orphans, but because the doctor was on the governing body of the grim grey building in which they were housed he never lost an opportunity to attack the administration. Half suffocated inside the brown paper, I struggled helplessly.

"If you're nae wantin' tae hae me back tae sign a death certificate, mebbe you'd better mak some holes in yon parcel, tae let in the air," the doctor said, and quickly slammed the door behind him.

* * *

My father's own childhood had been extremely harsh. The elder of two brothers, he had been rejected by his mother, who idolized the younger boy. Many years later my own mother told me that when she had accepted his proposal of marriage he had wept, so unable had he been, up to that moment, to believe that anyone could love him. He confided to her that his earliest memories were of hiding his head under his pillow so as to conceal his misery when — as always happened — his mother kissed his brother goodnight and then left the room without even approaching his own bed; his father also treated him with the utmost severity. Neither parent ever gave him a present either at Christmas or on his birthday, and when at the age of 13 he went to Eton his parents neither visited him nor allowed him to come out for such school festivities as the cricket match between Eton and Harrow, which was held annually in London and to which all the boys traditionally went. Nor did his life much improve as he grew older, for although he joined a dashing regiment — the 12th Lancers — his father gave him no allowance, with the result that although his brother-officers liked him and nicknamed him Remedy (short for 'Remedy-for-the-blues'), he was continually teased about money; his friends, knowing the size of his father's estate, simply could

67

not believe that he had no income other than his pay — in those days very small — and they looked on his refusal to order wine with his meals as a sign of eccentricity.

He was, however, much respected as a soldier, and when in 1902 he was created a Companion of the Distinguished Service Order, thirty lines of closely-packed type recorded his outstanding military career. Retiring from the army in 1909 — the year he married my mother — he rejoined at the start of the 1914 war and, until severely wounded, commanded a highland regiment. After my grandfather made over the estate to him, he did everything in his power to be a good landlord; he was hard-working and honourable, and no doubt did everything with the very best intentions, but perhaps because he had never known affection from his own parents he found it almost impossible to show love to his children. True, when the boys were away at school he sat down at his big roll-top desk every Sunday, to write to them, and when my nearest sister, tripping over a dog, fell hands-first into a blazing fire she found herself — in terrible pain — being cradled consolingly in his arms. But the only time I ever remember him playing with me was when he once showed me how to tie a fisherman's knot, and as soon as I had mastered the intricacies of fastening line to cast he sent me brusquely away. Whether because he was in continual pain from his war-wound — which had torn away much of the muscles of his right arm — or because he was already developing the hardening of the arteries from which he died, he was an unapproachable father, and when someone finally broke the news to me of his death, I was at a loss to know why it seemed expected of me that I should cry.

Although I don't doubt that he loved her deeply, he showed little understanding or consideration towards my mother. Even after the estate had been made over to him, my grandfather and my grandmother continued to live in the castle, bickering so continually with each other that my mother, pregnant for the second time, felt driven to have the baby in a rented house; my father, bringing her home with the heir (her first child had been a girl) in her arms, was embarrassed to find that the tenants had stretched a banner of welcome across the drive, and were gathered in the forecourt of the castle to cheer. Ordering the chauffeur to stop the car, he jumped out, leaving my mother to arrive at the door alone. Even if his action was caused by the fundamental shyness that may have lain under his apparently total self-confidence, it was not a kind thing to do, and though nothing could seriously damage my mother's devotion to him the incident was one which she never forgot.

My father never joined in any of our treats, such as our winter visits to the pantomime, or birthday teas. Each year, the theatre in the market town put on a Christmas production of Dick Whittington or Cinderella or Humpty Dumpty or — to us wonderful, because of the flying — Peter Pan. My mother booked seats in the front row of the dress circle, with an extra, unoccupied seat to put our coats on. The manager of the theatre, resplendent — even though we always attended a matinee — in dinner-jacket and black tie, met us at the door, bowed to mother as if she was royalty, and personally ushered us to our places. Pantomimes, in those days, were truly designed for children, with none of the adult-orientated vulgarities that later crept in; as the fabulous stories unfolded, I was torn between wishing the afternoon would never end and longing for the most magical moment of all — the transformation scene that ritually terminated the performance.

Even before I could count, I looked forward eagerly to my birthday, marking off the days on the nursery calendar by a simple before-breakfast progression from one square to the next. My birthday was for me a magic day — the one day in the year on which I was completely confident that I would not be either scolded or smacked. Of course, if I was naughty on my birthday I would no doubt have been chastised, but whoever heard of anyone being naughty on their birthday? On my birthday I could do more or less what I wanted, I could choose the pudding for luncheon (almost always opting for pink jelly) and could even be fairly sure that the grown-ups would actually listen to me if I wanted to tell them something. Under such heavenly circumstances, who could possibly sin?

Birthday presents were few and, on the whole, practical. My father didn't think much of toys; for my sixth birthday, therefore, he and my mother gave me a school desk, and for my seventh I received a set of carpentry tools. These were not toy tools, but full-sized workmen's ones; I had to take both hands even to lift the hammer.

The present I liked best was a doll made from a stocking, which I was given when I was four; she had black boot-button eyes, and because she was bald she wore, whether naked or dressed, a pink crocheted bonnet. Her name was Cuddly, and I loved her dearly, but when I was six an over-officious nanny, deciding that she was dirty, cremated her in the nursery fire. All that remained were the two boot-button eyes and the hook off her bonnet. I was heartbroken, and even the gift from a sympathetic visitor of a china doll with real hair could not console me. I was almost glad

when the visitor's own child resentfully stamped on the head of my new doll; if Cuddly could not — phoenix-like — be re-born I did not want a substitute and, indeed, I never had another doll.

The morning I was given Cuddly, a pink ribbon had been uncomfortably knotted into my stubbornly straight hair, and I had been sent to visit my mother in her bedroom. My father always got up early, but my mother, who never quite succeeded in adjusting herself to either the cold or the spartan habits of the north, lay in bed for as long as she dared, sipping China tea and nibbling very thin slices of white bread and butter. It was lucky for her that she had not married into an earlier generation of the family, for about 1734 one of my ancestors had written of his young wife — like my mother, from the south — that she was 'a dreadful slug-a-bed; Tis oft six of a morn ere she rises'.

I knocked at my mother's door, and the little wheels of the pulley squeaked as she released the fastener. "Come in!" she called, and I reached up for the handle. It was of porcelain, painted with forget-me-nots, and in the chilly air of the passage it felt like a lump of ice.

My birthday was in December, so there was a fire burning in her bedroom, the reflection of the flames licking brightly against the shiny brass fireguard. On the fur hearth-rug stood a circular metal bath, to which the maids would later carry hot-water cans shaped like tall tea-pots, my mother having refused to bathe anywhere except in front of her bedroom fire. Not for her the rigours of the castle's only bathroom, from the hot taps of which — or so the story went — ice had been known to fall. In later years, she spent another part of her dowry in adding more bathrooms to the castle — a visitors' bathroom, a maids' bathroom, a schoolroom bathroom, and a bathroom for the nursery, but they, too, were linoleum-floored and bleak, and were used more from a sense of duty

71

than from any expectation of pleasure.

My mother was sitting up in her princess-and-the-pea bed, propped against a pile of lace-edged pillows; she wore a frilled georgette bedjacket, and her yard-long brown hair streamed down on to the silk-covered eiderdown. She held out her arms to me.

"Happy Birthday! Have some sugar!" And she proffered a lump of sugar from her tray, her hand held flat, as if I were a pony.

I climbed up beside her, feet tucked under the eiderdown.

"And how old are you today? Is it one, or two?"

I giggled happily, and slid down until only my nose was clear of the eiderdown. Secretly, I licked the silk; it tasted, disappointingly, of nothing.

"Three, then?"

I shrieked with laughter, and rolled over and over, down into the hollow from which my father had risen.

"Surely you can't be *four*? Not *already*?"

My mother's black terrier, woken unexpectedly from a dream of chocolate-peppermint-creams, jumped barking from his basket as I bounced up and down on the big bed, trying to grab from her the present that she had magically produced from under her pillows.

The high spot of a birthday was tea, which was served in the dining room. Balanced on a heap of cushions in my father's big chair I contemplated, entranced, the crackers and the tinsel and the chocolate biscuits, the shortbread and Swiss rolls and ginger snaps that spread in seemingly limitless bounty between me and my mother, at the other end of the table. On either side sat my brothers and sisters, for this one glorious day relegated to positions subservient to my own. Toward the end of tea, all the candles on the table were blown out and my birthday cake was brought in, its candles seeming to me to burn as brightly as the sun. Chocolate cake with white icing, the words 'Many Happy Returns' scrolled in pink around the top — had there ever been a more beautiful cake? Surely not, I told myself as, paper hat falling over my eyes, I licked some icing off my fingers, positively daring the grown-ups to correct my manners. Birthdays were always happy.

Christmas was another wonderful day. When my mother first came to the castle, she had been horrified to find that it was treated as an ordinary working day; she looked out of the window on the first Christmas morning of her marriage and was astounded to see the gardeners raking the gravel of the castle courtyard. Later in the day, she was amazed to discover the village shop open for trade and to find the blacksmith hammering noisily at an hour when she expected him to be on his knees in the kirk. The very next year, she set about importing the delights of Christmas, superimposing — like the early Apostles — new customs onto rites that already existed.

One of the ancient games that my mother found still being played in the castle was brandy snapping. Brandy snapping — the name came not from the drink but from the word 'brand', a derivation from the old verb 'brinnan', to burn — was in its original form played by standing all the young girls round a silver dish. This dish, about the size of a card table, was filled with nuts, which were then doused with spirits and set alight. The girls had to snatch the nuts from the flames, and burned fingers were once supposed to be a sign that a girl was no longer a virgin. The secret, of course, lay in snapping up a nut so quickly that the flames did not have time to strike. But seeing the anguish that this yearly joke caused young servant-girls who, completely virtuous, hesitated for the very understandable reason that they were frightened of fire — my mother widened the net and per-suaded everyone to play, infiltrating the idea that the girl who snatched the most nuts would be the first to marry. In the darkened dining room, the flames leaped up toward the rose-and-thistle ceiling as family, visitors and servants jostled round the lighted dish. If my father saw some young maid dithering on the edge of the group, he would pick her up bodily and force her hand into the flames. "Come on now! We can't have you ending up a spinster!" Struggling and screaming happily, she would allow her hand to be forced among the burning nuts, and would then be thrown through the air into the arms of whichever of the watching menservants seemed keenest to catch her.

Finding that there was a tradition of feasting and decorating the castle with evergreen boughs, she had little difficulty in adding to the day turkeys, plum puddings and Christmas trees, and although everyone continued to work on Christmas Day, Christmas presents appeared — not only in the castle but all over the estate. My mother kept a reference book in which she had written down the names and birth dates of all the tenants' children and the presents that she had previously given them, and about a month before Christmas she would take us shopping to help her select the current year's gifts. Back home, dolls, footballs, clasp knives, mouth organs, toy soldiers, conjuring sets and other toys were laid out on the billiard table, labelled carefully, and tied up in holly-decked paper. My mother made it a rule never to give the children of the tenants anything useful, thinking that their lives were quite serious enough already. When all the parcels were done up, she would have them loaded into big wicker baskets and piled in the back of the Daimler; then she would set off around the estate. As she stopped for a chat at each house, this delivery of the presents could take anything up to a fortnight.

The best known of all the Scottish festivals, that of Hogmanay, was not celebrated in the castle, my father only acknowledging the existence of the New Year's Eve revelry by allowing, as was common all over Scotland, New Year's Day itself to be taken as a fully paid holiday.

Besides Christmas, my mother's other winter innovation was the hockey party. In those days, the lairds, even though they might be close friends with their tenants, did not mix with them socially, nor did they extend much of a welcome to local professional people. This resulted in an acute lack of companionship for their daughters. Whether these girls were home only for the holidays or, lessons behind them, were living permanently in the widely separated castles, they rarely saw one another, and even more rarely had the chance of meeting young men. They whiled away the cold, dismal days with books or needlework, with practising the piano or taking the dogs for walks. Almost always, they were extremely lonely. My mother saw this and, trying to think of a way that a lot of young people could be entertained without too much trouble, hit on the idea of a hockey party. Hastening off to a school outfitters', she bought several dozen hockey sticks. She then engaged the local band (one elderly lady who played the piano, accompanied by her son on the accordion), ordered in a large quantity of food, and sent out invitations. From north, south, east and west, the young men and girls converged on the castle; those who were too young to drive were brought by their family chauffeurs, who were themselves glad of an outing. The young people arrived after lunch, warmly wrapped in a good many layers of wool, and were at once sent out to the big lawn behind the castle to join whichever team had fewer players. There were no rules, no umpire, and no half-time — anybody who was exhausted simply dropped out, and rejoined his team when he felt better. Whoever arrived after all the hockey sticks had been appropriated used a golf club, a walking stick, or his foot. The scrimmage went on till dark, when everyone tumbled indoors to gorge on hot buttered scones and thick, spoon-supporting cocoa.

Then, while the servants busied themselves clearing away the tea and laying the table for dinner, the girls and young men went upstairs, where, strictly segregated, they had baths. The spare rooms allocated to the girls were littered with discarded pullovers and muddy shoes; party dresses hung from curtain rails and cupboard doors, petticoats were flung over chairs, and a confusion of evening slippers and embroidered handbags lay jumbled on the sofas. Under the eiderdowns of the huge beds, laughing, gossiping groups of girls — supposed to be resting — hugged their knees and chattered as if in the space of a couple of hours they had to exchange every single thought that had ever passed through their heads.

At seven o'clock, the dressing gong boomed, and an hour later everyone was gathered in the dining room where extra chairs had been crammed round all the tables. In the light of the flickering candles, the faces of the fifty or sixty young people who were seated at dinner glowed with excitement. That evening there seemed no such thing as an ugly girl.

In the Big Drawing Room, my mother had fixed a looking glass behind each of the wall brackets, so that it appeared that the room was lit by a hundred candles instead of fifty. Fires blazed in the fireplaces, the long curtains were tightly drawn — shutting out the blackness of the night — the furniture was pushed against the damask-hung walls, the carpets rolled back. The pianist struck a commanding chord on the piano, while her son wrestled the first note out of his accordion.

Up and down the shining parquet we raced, Strip the Willow, the Dashing White Sergeant, eightsome reels, foursome reels, sixteensome reels, the Duke of Perth, and Petronella — nobody dreamed of sitting out a single dance. One of my ancestresses had composed a strathspey that was known by the name of the castle, and this was always included in the evening's music. At midnight, the chauffeurs were summoned from their games of whist in the servants' hall, hot soup was handed around, and sheepskin coats were thrown over evening clothes. Missing girls emerged, bright-eyed, from unexpected corners, to be followed seconds later by self-conscious young men. Addresses were scribbled on starched shirt cuffs, and promises for future meetings exchanged. Half-frozen engines spluttered in the courtyard, car doors slammed, and red tail-lights vanished down the drive.

After that first hockey party, I went up to my bedroom in the tower too excited to sleep. It had been used as one of the changing-rooms for the girls; I opened the window to let out the warm, powder-scented air, and leaned on the sill, gazing into the darkness. About a quarter of a mile away I could dimly discern the oblong of the Camp Field, so named because, in 1307, King Robert the Bruce had camped there with his army. The ghosts of the soldiers who had died soon after in the savage Battle of Barra were too weary with age to haunt; the winter night was utterly silent — no dog barked, no owl screeched in the frozen forests. Then suddenly, like a vast golden curtain, the aurora borealis swept along the northern horizon. For a moment, the lights hung motionless, then they wavered and changed to pink. It seemed that I heard a sharp sound, like the crack of a whip — could it have come from the sky, or could it have been that the shifting lights, recalling to my subconscious the chromatic cloaks of clowns, gave me the impression that I was the solitary spectator of some stupendous celestial circus, commanded by a spectral scarlet-coated ringmaster? But as the sound - — whether real or imaginary — ricocheted away down the ice-fringed river, the lights in the sky changed to mauve and blue and then, shifting sideways, dissolved, to reappear a moment later in stripes of brightest silver. For several minutes, a hundred miles from the surface of the earth, the lights shifted, forming and re-forming in columns and ribbons and draperies of ever-changing colours, and then, as suddenly as they had appeared, they vanished, and I was left rubbing my eyes, half dazed with sleep and wondering if the whole vision had been a dream. I stumbled into bed, and pulled the eiderdown up around my ears. In the dark silence, I heard the rats scampering through the wainscoting as they hurried downstairs to search for their share of the feast.

The hockey party was such a success that all through the Christmas and Easter holidays parties like it were given in the neighbouring castles, the sticks being moved around to whichever laird was to be host to the week's game. Their summer equivalent, though on a smaller scale, was the tennis party. Resigned to the impossibility of persuading my father to spend money on anything that he personally considered inessential, my mother had sold some of her treasured books to provide a hard court, which gave my sisters a distinct advantage over other girls, whose parents' grass courts hardly had time for their first mowing before they were again threatened with snow. On Sunday afternoons, white-trousered young men, home from Oxford or Cambridge, would climb out of strap-bonneted sports cars and, to my eyes looking impressively sophisticated and elegant, would sip homemade lemonade under the lime trees that flanked the court as they waited their turn to exhibit their prowess before the admiring girls. Occasionally, the proceedings were enlivened still further by the arrival of foreign young men, sent to Britain to improve their English. The hard tennis court served a double function — in winter it could be flooded, and used for ice hockey; those of us who were too small to join in pushed each other about the ice on wooden kitchen chairs, hugging the encircling netting.

In winter we also went ski-ing. Even the most watery sun

would, when its rays were reflected by miles of unbroken snow, provide enough light to guide us as we searched the lofts for skis. These skis were long, heavy, and rigid — not mountain skis but trekking skis, made for traversing the flat wastes of the Arctic. At the ski runs, we strapped them onto our heavily-nailed winter boots and, having read more about Switzerland than about Scandinavia, precipitated ourselves down the slopes. Nobody taught us how to turn or stop — we just plunged downhill until we either reached the bottom or fell.

But to reach our ski-runs, we had to journey again through darkness — the darkness of the pine-forests on the lower slopes of the hills. Little snow and still less light penetrated the bushy tops of the closely-planted trees, while underfoot the fallen pine-needles of past years, deepest green rotting into black, muffled the sound of our steps. We might have been swimming in some subaqueous cavern, the sky above the tree-tops roofing us like the surface of water seen from deep under the sea.

Soon after three o'clock in the afternoon, the sun began to sink and, as if to make up in the last half hour for its shortcomings during the day, nearly always produced a magnificent sunset. Hurrying home, we would see the western sky spattered with orange and vermilion, the undersides of the clouds ablaze with scarlet. Pink and grey and clearest lemon-yellow, the high cirrus filaments streamed in the upper reaches of the air. Sombre against the gold of the horizon, homing rooks cawed their way to their untidy nests in the village beeches. Ahead of us would stretch another seemingly interminable winter evening. Once the wooden shutters were unfolded over the windows, and the heavy curtains — velvet, brocade, or flowered chintz, according to the category of the room they decorated, all both lined and interlined to keep out the cold — were drawn, we were, as far as entertainment was concerned, thrown back on our own resources.

Except on Sundays — when the only recreation allowed was making clothes or toys for the orphanage — we played cards, favouring the noisy grabbing types of games, in which the adroit use of an untrimmed finger-nail could ensure the capture of a coveted card. Or we clustered round my elder brother, as he moved the cat's-whisker of his home-made wireless from place to place on the crystal, and begged to be allowed a turn with the head-phones so as to hear, for a magical instant, the crackling sound of an infinitely-distant voice, or the tinny notes of a far-away, other-world piano. Sometimes we joined the grown-ups in the Big Drawing Room, to make our own music — my mother playing the violin, my nearest sister the piano, and my elder brother the flute; my second brother, anxious to take part but as yet without his future musical ability, played a tin whistle, his small fingers splayed resolutely over what he hoped were the right holes.

From the lofts we hauled down hampers of outdated clothes and disused screens faced with damask or embossed wall-paper or collages of Victorian or Edwardian pictures, carefully snipped from long-vanished magazines. We dressed up, and using the screens to form wings, backdrop and front curtain, acted plays which — because we had written them ourselves — had parts for everyone, including the dogs. A poker sword flashed as a Greek hero, inviolate behind a breast-plate conjured from a silver-sequinned Lanvin bolero, did battle with a monster — its height alarmingly increased by the sable muff that rested on top of its ears — for possession of a wilting maiden, lashed to an Andromeda-rock chair by the ribbons of her bizarrely over-long Molyneux ball-dress.

We invented many ways of passing the long evenings, but

80

above all, we read. Not having learnt to read until I was seven, I was something of a disgrace in the family; it didn't seem to occur to anyone that the process of learning was, for me, complicated by the fact that I was being taught by a French governess who, herself confused by the inconsistencies of such English words as 'cough', 'ought' and 'bough', had scant patience with a child who seemed incapable of distinguishing between, for instance, a simple French word such as 'il' and the figure eleven. Il . . . 11 . . . Il . . . 11 . . . no matter how hard I tried, I could see no difference between the two pairs of symbols and, believing me to be not only stupid but also stubborn, my governess refused to explain; her ebony ruler, shaped like a skinny rolling-pin, tapped first the French reading primer, then the arithmetic book, and finally — with petulant force — my knuckles.

Finally, however, I learnt — and immediately became passionately addicted to books. Like a clothes-moth concealed in a chest of blankets, I devoured everything within reach and, our nursery books being limited to Beatrix Potter, A.A. Milne, and a few volumes of fairy stories — all of which, from having had them read to me, I already knew by heart — I quickly moved on to the ones that had survived from my mother's childhood — *Robin's Ride, My Neighbour's Shoes, Mademoiselle Pourquoi, The Dove In The Eagle's Nest, Les Malheurs De Sophie*, and a stirring epic called *Detained In France*, which had, appropriately enough, been given to my grandmother for her birthday when, in 1870, she and her parents had been pinned down on the far side of the Channel by the Franco-Prussian war. Then it was the turn of my brothers' out-grown favourites — *The Trail Of The Sandhill Stag, Two Little Savages, The Call Of The Wild,* and *Scouting For Boys*, but soon exhausting the possibilities of building fir-branch tepees and of following paw-marks through the muddier patches of the woods, I turned my attention to my

81

mother's library in the guard tower and worked my way doggedly through Dickens and Kipling and Scott, interspersed with Dante's *Inferno* — illustrated in chilling detail by Gustave Doré — and bound volumes of Punch.

I read anywhere and everywhere; curled up in my father's big arm-chair — whose high back, designed to keep off draughts, formed an effective barrier against interruptions — in the bath, on horseback, in chapel (the book disguised inside the Jesus-decorated dust-jacket of my bible), and up trees, but especially in bed at night. Our candles were blown out early and we were forbidden to re-light them, but carefully-hoarded pennies could buy batteries for electric torches and I read nightly with my head under the blankets, ears alert for the footfalls of grown-ups who, if they came in unexpectedly, might spot the tell-tale glow; it was, in fact, rather more comfortable to read with the blankets pulled over my head, for in winter the cold in my bedroom was so severe that even to have my fingers above the covers could be quite painful. Dying torch-batteries had their usefulness prolonged by periods of rest — two minutes of reading, with the faint light fading to nothingness, followed by a minute with the torch switched off, during which it miraculously regained its strength. Then two more minutes of reading, eyes racing over the page before the words again became invisible. Then another minute of recuperation, and finally the despairing moment when no amount of rest would revive the battery, and there was nothing for it but to drop the book on the floor and wait for sleep.

As a variant to reading, I wrote. Seated at my birthday-present desk in the deep embrasure of the schoolroom window — the walls of the castle were, at this level, about six feet thick, so the desk fitted easily between room and panes — I would fill exercise-book after exercise-book with adventure stories, the plots modelled on those of John

82

Buchan and Robert Louis Stevenson. With no direct know-ledge of the outside world, I drew my backgrounds from random facts gleaned from books of travel and geography, and when, made rash by the excitement of creation, I showed my work to grown-ups the inevitable inconsistencies made them laugh. Discouraged, I abandoned writing, and did not attempt it again for nearly forty years.

The acquisition of the necessary knowledge was made especially difficult by the fact that, outside the schoolroom, I was rationed to one question a day. Our reference books were limited and, lessons seldom covering the subjects that really interested me, I was torn by the daily decision of whether to ask, for instance, why the moon waxed and waned, or whether to squander my precious question on, perhaps, the welfare of an absent dog. Sometimes I inadvertently phrased an unimportant remark in the form of a question, and on subsequently presenting a carefully-thought-out query, would laughingly be told that I had already used up my day's ration. It was indeed laughingly — not harshly — that my parents refused to answer me; they looked on my curiosity as mildly amusing, but also as something that should not — because it was a nuisance to grown-ups — be indulged.

The convenience of the grown-ups was all-important. No doubt my father and mother felt a normal parental love for us children — my mother, in fact, once refused an invitation to visit America with my father, believing that both of them should not be such a long sea-voyage away from home at the same time. (She admitted later that she was almost sorry that none of us had fallen ill while my father was away, so she could, in fact, quite safely have gone with him.) But in spite of their undoubted concern, three of the twelve indoor ser-vants — if one can count a governess as a kind of servant — were employed for the sole purpose of making sure that my parents had as little as possible to do with us.

83

In my entire childhood, for instance, I only once remember my mother giving me my bath — if it was Nanny's afternoon off, then the nursery-maid was always there to check that the water was hot enough — but not too hot — and that my rubber sponge was liberally lathered with Pears transparent soap. (Natural sea-sponges were never soaped; the coarse-pored ones, as big as footballs, were used to splash water over one's body, while the small fine-pored ones were used to wash one's face.) My mother, who genuinely cared about the happiness of the servants, spent much time and trouble on making sure that they were well looked after and contented. Indeed, she confided to me, when I was older, that what she had really wanted was to have retired eventually with my father to one of the modern bungalows that had been built in the suburbs of the county town; there, she thought she could have managed without domestic help, and it would, she imagined — after so many years spent trying to sort out her servants' personal problems — have been heaven to have been preoccupied with nobody's worries but her own. But meanwhile, such were the customs of the day that it never seemed to have occurred to her that all the time and energy she spent on caring for the servants who in turn cared for her children might perhaps have been more rewardingly spent in caring for the children herself.

On Sundays we saw slightly more of our parents, because we went with them to church. Our family had a different religion from that of the people who lived on the estate, for we belonged to the Episcopalian church, whereas they were Presbyterians. Once a month a fat itinerant minister with dyed red hair visited us and held a service in our damp private chapel, but on three Sundays out of four we went to the Presbyterian kirk in the village.

By the time I was born, the kirk had been in continuous

84

use as a place of worship for over seven hundred and fifty years; its bible, the tattered-edged leaves yellowed with age, belonged to the days of Charles II, and its communion register went back to 1630. When I was still quite small, restoration work on it revealed a perfect Norman arch, but — oblivious to its history — we children preferred the kirk simply because the form of service held there incorporated ad-lib prayers from the minister; mostly these were intercessions on behalf of sick or bereaved members of the congregation, but there was always a hope that the minister would pray for the salvation of a sinner, especially if the sinner's identity was not too difficult to guess.

If bored by the length of the sermon, my father would pull out his fob watch. This — hung on a gold chain which, threaded through a button-hole, spanned his waistcoat from pocket to pocket — was of the type known as a 'repeater', and when a button on top of its winder was pressed would chime not only the hour but also announce — by one, two or three notes of a higher pitch — the quarter hours. If the minister ignored this discreet but clearly audible reminder my father would leave our front-row family pew and ostentatiously poke the coals of the iron stove that was the kirk's only heating or, if the weather was warm, fetch a hook-ended pole from the vestry and noisily adjust the sashes of the tall arch-topped windows. Perhaps he felt an unconscious sense of unity with the congregation that had listened in this same kirk to the sermons of John Wesley, who wrote in 1766, after his third visit, "I spoke exceedingly plain; yet the hearers did not appear to be any more affected than the stone walls."

On summer Sundays, the door of the kirk might be left open, giving me glimpses of patient dogs, waiting outside for their worshipping — and worshipped — masters. Fidgeting on our too-upright pew, I would while away the time by studying the memorial stones of my ancestors; set high into the granite walls, these stone pages chronicled not only their lives but also the circumstances of their deaths.

One recorded the brief life of a midshipman, lost at sea. Always lonely, I wished that he could have been my friend, not fully realising that, had he survived the shipwreck, he would by then have been about 140 years old. Like the young men who, shortly before my birth, had died in the 1914–18 war, he seemed to live on, disembodied, in a mythical aura of perpetual youth.

Sailors were something of a rarity in my father's family, in contrast to that of my mother; on her side, as well as the great-great-grandfather who commanded the fleet to which Napoleon surrendered, I had a great-grandmother who had been brought up on a battleship. Her own mother (the result of a union, unblessed by the church, between one of the daughters of George III and a highland gentleman at court) having died when she was a baby, her father — at that time a captain, although later, like the other great-great-grandfather, an admiral — took her everywhere with him on his ship. My own mother remembered her well — she was, of course, my mother's grandmother — and often told me how that little girl's great joy had been to stand in the prow of her father's ship as, all sails spread, it cut through the waves. The drone of the minister's voice mingled stupefyingly with the buzz of a bumble-bee, trapped on the inner side of one of the kirk's plainly-glazed windows, but in my imagination both sounds were drowned by the roar of surf and the hiss of wind through taut rigging.

Against the eastern end of the kirk a high-walled roofless enclosure, once part of the chancel, had served until the time of my grandfather as a family burial-ground. Once, finding the key of its small, iron-studded door — which had some-how got attached to a bunch labelled School Trunks And Ferret Boxes — I turned the lock and leant fearfully against

86

the darkened timber. The door creaked open, revealing a shut-in wilderness of withered leaves, abandoned birds' nests, and weeds grown eerily, unnaturally tall. I did not linger to study the grave-stones.

Outside in the main church-yard, time-eroded grave-stones, moved from their original places to make room for subsequent generations of the dead, stood ranked in line against the south wall of the kirk, their weathered inscriptions only decipherable when the sinking sun, slanting across their surfaces, gave fleeting definition to the fast-vanishing incisions.

Friday was another day on which we saw more of our parents, because it was market-day in the county town. Until 1720 there had been no road between the castle and the town, but now there were two, and my father drove the Daimler in to attend to the business of the County Council, of which he was a diligent member, and to meet his friends for luncheon at his club. My mother went so as to leave a lengthy shopping-list at a superior grocer, who supplied goods that she could not get from the village shop, to do other more amusing shopping, and to lunch with *her* friends at the women's club, conveniently situated over the grocer's shop. We children were dragged, sick with fear, to the dentist; the water in the locality was very soft, and though my mother tried to add extra lime to our diet we often had holes in our teeth. Dentists, in those days, hurt, and as we were not allowed even to mention this to the dentist the strain of pretending to be brave added to that of enduring the pain.

We were also dragged, hardly less reluctantly, to the dancing-class. The floor of the room in which we were initiated into the arts of curtseying, bowing, pirouetting, chassé-ing and setting to partners was polished to a glassy smoothness, making it difficult for me, in my elastic-banded dancing-pumps, to keep my balance. Pink-faced with

87

embarrassment, I slithered round the room, acutely conscious that my handed-down dancing-dress fitted me only where it touched. My partner, a freckle-faced imp whose father shared with my own the dubious reputation of being the joint worst child-beaters in the county, got rid of his pent-up hatred of dancing — and possibly also the unconscious resentment he may have felt towards his father — by lying down in the middle of the floor and screaming.

When we were slightly older we sometimes managed to slip away to the cinema; in the afternoon all seats were reduced in price, which meant that we could lose ourselves in fantasies of Tarzan or Ben Hur for about the cost of two small bars of chocolate, or approximately a fortnight's spending-money. And once a year we were all lined up for a group photograph; frozen above unaccustomedly-neat clothes, our mutinous faces — recorded on sepia paper — revealed only too clearly what we thought of the ordeal. An early photograph shows me with one cheek unnaturally bulged, my elder brother having instructed me to push my tongue into it at the moment when — head concealed under a square of black cloth — the harassed photographer besought us all to watch the birdie. On the way home, the car would be halted, and the chauffeur — stiff-limbed in his heavy serge uniform — would climb out to light the head-lamps. From a snug nest among the fur motoring-rugs I would glimpse his face, momentarily lit from beneath by the flare of matches, and when later the car swept between the square granite pillars of our front gates I would do my best to feign sleep, hoping for the luxury of being carried upstairs to bed.

Our parents never went on holiday with us. For my elder brothers and sisters, just being at home from boarding-school was considered holiday enough, but my nearest sister and I were sent to a small seaside town for a fortnight of each summer term. Our governess went with us, as did our

88

lesson-books. Installed in a boarding-house run by the retired butler and cook from another castle, we put up with punctilious morning lessons before being walked — always in an orderly way — to the sea-shore.

This sea-shore was a never-ending source of delight, for not only could we build sand-castles on its damp golden inlets, but in its rock-pools we could watch a great variety of marine life. Scrambling carefully over the seaweed-draped rocks — so as to avoid stepping with bare feet on white acorn-barnacles or coolie-hat-shaped limpets — we would peer eagerly into the pools that had been left behind by the ebbing sea. Small crabs scuttled sideways, paused, stood for an instant on tiptoe, and scuttled on again; sea anemones — blue, green, pink or red — waved their feathery tentacles in seductive search of plankton or prawn; five-armed scarlet starfish stalked unsuspecting cockles; transparent shrimps tested the hardly-moving water with almost-invisible antennae, and from caverns only inches high the tentacles of tiny octopuses reached gropingly for prey. We laid streamers of bladder-wrack on jetties and jumped on them to pop the air-sacs, or filled our sandcastle-buckets with the wet shells of tellins and periwinkles and whelks — which looked disappointingly dull when dry. As we hunted for cuttlebones to carry home to our sisters' canaries, we might spot far down the shore — where the rocks ended and flat sand began — a solitary turnstone scurrying on busy red legs, first hastening inland and then seaward as it followed the edge of the advancing and retreating waves. Once we saw the Atlantic fleet leave a harbour on the opposite side of the firth; in line astern, magnificent and sinister, the great grey ships prowled out to sea. And on another day, when the skies — as grey as had been the warships — precluded games on the beach, our governess hired the local taxi and took us to Culloden, which lay not far behind the town.

89

This grim moor, the scene of the final defeat of Bonnie Prince Charlie, seemed never to have shaken off the anguish of that terrible battle. Even without closing my eyes, I could imagine the ragged, desperate ranks of the highlanders, struggling with their outdated swords against the solid, musket-armed ranks of the English. The wind, cutting coldly over the treeless upland, seemed to carry within it echoes of the screams of the fallen, and even the twisted heather seemed to smell, when I touched it, less of blossom than of blood. It was indeed a terrible place, to which I never wanted to return. Jolting back to the boarding-house in the old taxi, I remembered that we still had, in the castle, the sword that my ancestor had carried at Culloden; it hung on a hook on the spiral stairs and had last been worn at Buckingham Palace by my grandfather, when he accompanied my father and mother to court shortly after their marriage.

Even on holiday, we were not encouraged to make friends with other children. In the stunted jungle of gorse and broom that splayed over the beach-edge dunes we played mettlesome games of hide-and-seek with children who, because their names remained unknown, had for us all the mystery of a band of leprechauns. Emerging at length from our games — to find our governess knitting, oblivious, beside a breakwater — we would trail back to yet another boarding-house luncheon of mince and blancmange, never speaking of the playmates whose companionship we had so warily enjoyed.

The boarding-house had a small back garden. Used as we were to having almost limitless space around us, its Lilliputian confines fascinated us. With paces no longer than heel-to-toe we explored the miniature rockery, on the winding paths of which we could — within the length of a single fallen sunflower — unwind the golden road to Samarkand. The pebble-ringed goldfish pond stirred easily into a

*From a portrait of my mother
by G. Goddard Jackson, 1912*

Charybdis whirlpool, on which Odysseus, lashed to the match-stick mast of a walnut-shell barque, cried in a shrill six-year-old voice for succour from his gods. From the shade of an apple-tree came the muted tapping of fork against basin as the elderly cook, watching us with a benevolent eye, beat the remnants of a pink jelly into a supper-time mousse; enclosed in a lapped-larch fence, her garden was at once magical and secure, in many ways more suited to the desires of a child than the sometimes menacing grounds that surrounded the castle.

*   *   *

My mother, who didn't do many of the things she might have been expected to do, did others that were quite surprising. There was no hairdresser in the village — the local girls, planning to go to an evening 'social', would walk about all day with their hair in curlers, by tacit agreement invisible — so my mother cut the hair of all her family, including that of my father. A rug in the Big Drawing Room was rolled up and an old sheet put down in its place; armed with one pair of straight scissors and a second — with blades like a comb — that cut alternate strands, she would seat us in turn on a delicate gilded chair and, snipping with bravura, reduce our locks to something approaching civilised length. She made all the woollen knee-length socks worn by my father and my brothers, incorporating into their tops elaborate designs of cables or, for the evening, tartan; she could 'turn the heel' of these socks without looking, and often worked on them when reading some classic book to my elder brothers and sisters while — for the good of their postures — they lay flat on their backs on a hard parquet floor.

My mother had learnt to read upside-down at the age of four; her sister, two years older, was being taught by a governess and my mother, thought to be too young to join in,

had been seated on the far side of the table, ostensibly colouring pictures but in fact absorbing, in reverse, everything that her sister was being taught. Soon she had gone on to working out rudimentary Latin from the headings of psalms, and later, aided by foreign governesses, she rapidly mastered French, German and Italian. A keen reader not only in these languages but also in her own, she lost no time, after she married my father, in starting a village library. Housed in a room of one of the cottages near the shop, this was largely stocked with books from her own shelves, and was much patronised by the people of the estate who, with little else to divert them in the long evenings, read avidly.

When we were ill, mother would read to us by the hour or, as convalescence advanced, teach us to knit or crochet. Even my elder brother could knit — it passed the time for him when later, as a subaltern in the army, he fell on his head at a point-to-point and was forbidden for several weeks to read. She would always climb the spiral stairs to say goodnight to us before she went in to dinner; blankets pulled up under our chins, we would watch her glide in, her serene face lit from below by the glass-shaded candle in her hand. Before kissing us she would turn our pillows, so that our warm cheeks rested against linen that was both smooth and cool. She always wore a double row of pearls, and a diamond butterfly or diamond arrow pinned to the front of her dress; often there would be a diamond crescent tucked into her abundant hair, and always she smelt of lilies-of-the-valley.

I was too young to go with her to the evening meetings of the Women's Rural Institute, a monthly gathering of the women of the estate, but I loved going shopping with her, for she had engaging habits such as taking with her, when she went to buy a teapot, a bottle of water, so that she could make sure that her intended purchase would pour in a drip-free curve. It was fun, too, to help her give out the linen or the stores. The linen was kept in floor-to-ceiling cupboards in the housekeeper's room, and each department of the castle had to give her a written-out list of its needs. The shelves of the cupboards, like the drawers that held my father's clothes, were all neatly labelled; Sheets — double linen; Sheets — sides-to-middle; Bathtowels — visitors; Bathtowels — dogs and boys. These last were the bath towels that consisted more of darns than of original cloth; they were allocated to my brothers' bathroom and were also used for drying the dogs when they came in wet from shooting. My brothers said they didn't mind sharing towels with the dogs but did rather object to the dogs being put before them on the labels, even though, more than a hundred years before, a distant relation of ours had been overheard ordering her servants to "put on the porridge for the pigs and bairns" — the pigs, as more useful, coming first. The label 'sides-to-middle' on the shelf of sheets meant that the sheets were ones which, having been worn out down the centre, had been ripped in half and the two relatively strong sides sewn together by hand, making a serviceable object which — because of the joint that now ran down the centre — was not very comfortable to lie on, but which could be used for several more years.

The heads of the departments — Nanny, the butler, the cook, and the head housemaid — also presented lists of other things that they needed. Each list was made out in a small

94

note-book, so that my mother could — if she wanted — check back to see that no extravagance was taking place, for extravagance in any form was frowned on. The store room — later made into a ground-floor bathroom — from which these were given out was lined with shelves, holding enough dry goods to stock a small shop. Commodities such as sugar were bought by the sack, soap by the hundredweight, and candles by the gross, but if mould grew on top of a pot of jam, it was simply scraped off and the jam, after a quick re-boil, was transferred to a clean pot; wafer-thin ends of soap were collected and melted down for washing the floors, and old envelopes specially saved so that their backs could be used for writing down messages. In the cornucopian abundance of the store room I forgot all econmies, and, happily busy, counted out boxes of matches, or dribbled a golden stream of syrup from a gallon crock into a lidded Meissen jar.

Caring, as she did, so much for the welfare of the people around her, it was ironic that one of my mother's personal burdens was that there was virtually no place on the estate where she could be sure of privacy from them. Indoors, servants entered all rooms except bedrooms without knocking; outdoors, the 'policies', as the grounds around the castle were known, were laid out for effect rather than seclusion, so that as soon as she went outside she could be seen from a distance of about a mile. The kitchen garden was laid out in squares, so that no matter which path she took she was sure to be in view of a gardener. Go up any of the three drives, and she was fair game for the squirrel eyes of the village children, sent by their mothers to search under the beeches for kindling-sticks. Even the furthest fields and forests could conceal farm-hands and gamekeepers going quietly about their work, the clatter of their tackety boots muffled by plough-furrow or bracken. She could never be sure of being alone.

In desperation, she asked to have a secret garden. For several years my father managed to find excuses for not making one — the foresters were too busy, or the weather was wrong for sowing — but finally he gave in, and trees were felled to make a secluded oblong of lawn in a coniferous wood beyond the tennis court. Two garden seats were bought; one was placed at the end of the main path but the second was recessed into the garden's flanking firs, and on this she could actually rest with an almost-certainty of not being overlooked.

At the entrance to her garden my mother planted a briar rose. It was never trimmed, and soon developed the tangled enchantment of the Edmund Dulac roses that bowered my storybook's Sleeping Beauty; its small leaves smelled, when crushed between finger and thumb, like the expensive soap used by our exotic American aunt. My mother's garden always seemed to me to be lit by slanting evening sunlight, and filled with the soft coo-coo of drowsy doves.

Apart from her secret garden, only one other place was felt by my mother to be safe from watching eyes. This was a shady yew-enclosed spot just outside the small door by which she usually entered the high-walled kitchen garden. The head gardener, the garden boys, and all the main traffic of the garden went in and out by large double doors at the end of the farm yard, but my mother's door, reached from the front drive by a narrow path crossing a small rustic bridge, was so clandestine that I was convinced — wrongly — that it had been the model for the one depicted in *The Light Of The World*; after my father died, my mother confided to me that on the rare occasions when he went with her to the kitchen garden they used to pause in this small green haven, and kiss.

The kitchen garden provided not only all our vegetables and fruit, but also the flowers that were used to decorate the castle. In cold weather, terracotta pots planted with

96

begonias, chrysanthemums, cinerarias, euphorbias, fuschsias or pelargoniums would appear from the greenhouses, to be inserted into china or brass cache-pots or massed in lead-lined jardinières in the Big Drawing Room, the Little Drawing Room, the passages and the hall. In summer my elder sisters — the Girls — would drift to the kitchen garden in their sprigged cotton dresses and straw sun-hats, carrying flat wicker baskets which they would load with lupins and dahlias, roses and antirrhinums, calendulas, delphiniums, nigellas, scabious, phloxes, verbenas — anything and everything that was that day in perfect bloom. A sheet, similar to the one put down for hair-cutting, was spread, and on top of the grand piano in the Big Drawing Room and on other points of vantage they would construct extravagant pyramids and peacock-tail fans of flowers. My eldest sister was particularly good at flower-arranging; great sun-bursts of sweet peas, their colours flowing from deepest pink to rose to mauve to purple to blue, grew as if by magic under her fingers, scenting the rooms of the castle with a languorous midsummer sweetness.

This sister was also very skilled at embroidery, the backs of the canvases on which she worked presenting a neatness hardly distinguishable from that of the fronts. My second sister, doll-like in her rounded prettiness, was given to pinching and slapping anyone smaller than herself; perhaps a presentiment of how the Fates were going to squander both her looks and her talents was already brushing her naturally sweet nature with a nettle of baffled resentment. The sister who came next to me in the family — the other Child — was too close to me for me to see her clearly. I loved her unquestioningly and, although when we grew up we could no longer be much together, my feelings towards her never changed. My second brother — the younger Boy — was a more misty figure; away so much at school, he appeared to me mainly in

97

the role of satellite to the elder Boy. He came and went, conscientious, stubborn, and busy about his own affairs; I had to wait until we were both much older to learn and appreciate his many admirable qualities.

Of all his children, my elder brother presented the greatest challenge to my father, for he was exceptionally intelligent, gifted not only academically but also in the worlds of sport and music. My father, diligent but not intellectually clever, could see only one way to deal with this outstanding, rebellious boy, and that was — in the parlance of those days — to 'break his spirit'. Sent to Eton but not allowed by my father to take up the scholarship that he had won — for in my father's days at Eton scholarship boys, known as 'tugs', had been looked down on by the boys whose fathers could afford to pay fees — my brother was continually thrashed both at school and at home. He was even thrashed for leaping to the defence of my mother, when a local dignitary spoke rudely to her — deference to a senior member of the male sex, it seemed, ranking higher in my father's scale of values than a boy's natural loyalty to his mother. Destined to die in action in the second world war, my elder brother led a life that was, in many ways, sadly misunderstood.

*　　*　　*

When I was about six a telephone was put into the castle; its number, as befitted the first instrument in the neighbourhood, was 1, and I was terrified of it. Whoever was nearby when it rang was meant to answer it, but if I was alone when it made the little preliminary click that presaged a ring I would bolt from the room, praying that nobody would see me go, for whoever then had to run to answer it would be justifiably annoyed. The instrument stood upright, like a candlestick, and as well as the usual bottle-shaped listening-piece had a second circular one, to be pressed to the other ear of anyone who, from lack of familiarity with the apparatus, insisted that the voices that came over it were impossible to hear. This second ear-piece also allowed two people to listen to the same caller, an advantage in the eyes of my father who, outraged at seeing telephone poles march across his land, felt that if two of his family were listening for the price of one he was somehow getting his own back on the telephone company.

The telephone was a great blessing to my mother, who previously, if my father was late in returning from a journey, or even from a day out, had simply had to watch and wait until he appeared. My father's dog shared these anxious vigils with her; it seemed to have a mysterious intuition of his return, jumping onto a window-seat and looking eagerly up the drive long before the time when it could have heard the engine of the car. Telegrams travelled fast, and if my father was delayed in daytime he could usually let my mother know, but the suspense — even with the dog to keep her company — must have been nerve-racking in the hours of darkness.

Over a great part of my childhood there hung an aura of darkness. Not a metaphorical darkness of poverty or disease, for we were by most standards rich and by any standards healthy, but of real darkness — the actual physical lack of light. Although far south of the Arctic Circle, the district had much in common with the lands of the midnight sun, which meant, of course, that for half the year the days were extremely short.

In winter, we rose by starlight and did our before-breakfast piano practice by the light of candles. By nine o'clock, a sad red sun had crept bleakly over the horizon. Little of its light penetrated the deep-set windows of our school-room in the tower; we grew accustomed to holding our lesson books up above our heads, to take advantage of what small illumination there was, for even the shadow of our own shoulders was enough to make the text undecipherable. Strangely, none of us suffered from eyestrain; perhaps our pupils expanded in the gloom, like those of cats.

Blackest of all was the darkness inside the castle on the long winter evenings. No matter how many lamps were carried up from the lamp room, no matter how many candles were wedged, guttering, into polished candlesticks, there were still uncounted dark corners. Under tables, behind screens, in unlit fireplaces, behind drawn curtains, and around the bends in the long passages, we children knew malignant demons lurked. They lived, we believed, in almost every corner of the castle — anywhere, in fact, where it was dark. They crouched in unlit fireplaces, and under the half-opened lid of the big oak rug-box in the hall. They cackled up the echoing waste-pipe of the bath, and whined like hungry wolves in the draughts that whistled under the doors. On the backs of the scrambling rats they jockeyed satanic races, separated only by crumbling skirting-boards from my bedroom slippers, and bats — squeaking supersonically under their spurs — bore them vampire-like past wind-flurried casements. Though I was never frightened of the ghosts, I was scared stiff of the demons, and after I grew too old to be cared for by a nanny — losing, at the same time, the comfort of a final tuck-up from my mother — going to bed in the winter was a waking nightmare. I had dinner with the grown-ups in the dining-room, but immediately after, as they settled down by the Big Drawing Room fire, I had to say goodnight and set out on the terrifying journey to bed. First, I went out of the brightly lit Big Drawing Room, through the subdued lighting of the Little Drawing Room, and into the passage. This was where the fear began, for, with two doors now shut between us, I could no longer hear the voices of the people I had left behind; I started to climb the spiral

100

stairs. These were lit only by tiny oil nightlights, flickering at alternate twists of the spiral. One dark curve, one curve faintly lit, another dark curve — the stairs wound up and up. I reached my bedroom floor, and lit the candle which, in its saucered silver candlestick — complete with silver snuffer — I had picked up as I left the Little Drawing Room. At the rasp of the match, pointed ears pricked up, and small claws flexed with anticipation; the demons who were waiting for me had woken, and I would not be out of danger until I was actually in bed. I crossed an empty, unused bedroom, and at last gained the comparative safety of my own room; quickly I closed the door and laid the sand-filled draught-excluder along the bottom to silence the moaning of the wind, wondering if I could summon up the courage to go to the bathroom or whether this would be yet another night when my teeth remained unbrushed. A trailing branch of ivy tapped against the windowpane, soot pattered down onto the pleated-paper fan that stood in the unlit grate. Somehow, my dinner dress was always a little small for me, a fraction tight; it had to be pulled off over my head, and this, I was convinced, was the moment when a demon would get me; heart hammering, I tore off the dress before it had time to attack. My flannel nightdress — of the type known in the family as a 'fore and aft' because it was cut the same both front and back — was warm from the stone pig around which the maid had wrapped it. Safe in bed, I blew out the candle and resolutely shut my eyes.

Although inside the castle I was frightened of the dark, out of doors I felt completely happy. In the luminous nights of early spring, when the grown-ups thought I was safely in bed, I would slip out through a pantry window, squeezing easily between the iron bars, and run with my black Labrador through the woods. Under the towering beech trees, the dog would snuffle in the fallen beech masts as I paused, listening

101

for the owls and the faint, shrill cries of the hunting weasels. Sleeping pigeons stirred in the branches, while in the undergrowth nameless small creatures rustled and squeaked, hurrying about their nocturnal business. The wind blew through the bushes, but here it was not frightening — it was a friendly movement of air, bringing messages of opening leaves, of drowsy, cud-chewing cows, and eddying hints of dampness from the river. There was only one place where neither my dog nor I would go at night; that was the Druids' Circle, a miniature Stonehenge halfway down one of the drives. There were three such circles on the estate, all probably raised in the late neolithic or early bronze age. The seven stones of the one near the drive — on the edge of a field still known as The Druids — stood as they had done for more than three thousand years, gaunt under the scudding clouds of the night sky, the ferns around them strangely stunted, as if their tangled roots enmeshed a distant memory of shuffling sandalled feet. Even in daylight, I avoided this place.

In the summer, when the globe, like a seesaw, had tilted under our feet, everything changed, and instead of the endless nights there were apparently endless days. My elder sisters played tennis till nearly midnight, the *plack-plack* of the balls reaching me where I lay curled in my hammock between two trees of an avenue of limes. We all slept out of doors in the summer, as if to squeeze the ultimate drop of enjoyment from the brief warm weeks. With tents and hammocks, we established our summer territories on the lawns around the castle, watching from the snugness of woollen blankets the dawn follow the dusk with only brief twilight hours between. We went to sleep to the soft sound of an owl's flight as it skimmed over us, searching the grass for field mice, and woke to the distant cries of migrant oyster catchers, homing in to their nests by the river.

In summer, the river turned from a threatening torrent,

102

jagged with ice, into a cool, inviting stream. We paddled in the shallows or, secretly stripping off our clothes, swam naked in the salmon pools. The fish, which scattered if we splashed the surface of the water, had no fear if we entered quietly; under water, in the brown-stoned sun-speckled depths of the pools, fish and swimmers circled each other, mutually curious. The cart horses browsed and drowsed, hock-deep in the uncut grass of the water meadows, resting in the interval between plough and harvest. We treated their broad backs like sofas, lying on them, reading, through the long afternoons. The leather bindings of the books that we filched from my mother's library adhered conveniently to the warm hides of the horses, their faint mustiness mingling pleasantly with the scent of clover and the dubbined, stable smell of the horses' work-worn halters.

Late summer was the season of the Highland Games. Each district had its Games — a mixture of pageant, sports, and fair, eagerly looked forward to by everyone except the local policemen, who, between directing the traffic and frustrating the schemes of the gypsies, always had an extremely testing day. The proceedings opened with a parade of the clansmen, dressed to the nines in kilts and bonnets and plaids and any bit of old regalia they could lay their hands on. My father would have none of this; he looked on it as exhibitionism and leaned morosely on his tall shepherd's-crook stick, radiating disapproval, as the pipers, followed by the clansmen, marched around the ring.

Then came the sports — races and high jumping, long jumping, hammer throwing, putting the shot, and tossing the caber. This caber was a pine tree, stripped of its branches and bark; the competitor had to grasp it by its root end, heave it in the air so that, balanced on his hands, it stood as upright as it had done in the forest, and then toss it in such a way that it made a complete somersault, its topmost end skimming

103

the ground before it landed again on its lower end. There was wrestling, when the quarrymen took on the sheep-dippers, and dancing competitions, when — claymores crossed on the chalk-dusted boards of the boxing ring — tartan-clad stalwarts leaped and whirled in the intricacies of the sword dance. Outside the arena, the gypsies set up their swings and coconut shies, their candy-floss stalls and fortune-telling booths. Tartan-shawled, the women hawked ribbon-tied bunches of lucky white heather. Brown eyes bright with cunning, they noted into which pocket the farmer slipped his wallet, and passed the message on to a confederate at the crowded entrance to the tea tent.

Coming home triumphant, bearing in one hand the first-prize rosette gained by one of our dairy cows and in the other a bouncing gas-filled toy balloon, we would be greeted at the front door by the dogs, who had, much to their disappointment, been left behind. Three or four dogs usually lived inside the castle, and they had an endearing habit, which they passed on from generation to generation, of grasping a skirt hem or a coat-tail in their teeth and running along beside the wearer like a four-footed trainbearer. Each family homecoming turned into a procession as, led by my father with his kilt edge grasped in the jaws of his black Labrador, we were each escorted into the castle by a tail-wagging, hem-carrying dog.

In the front hall, my father would throw his bonnet onto the head of one of the carved angels that flanked the fireplace. These angels cropped up in the most unexpected places; in minuscule they stamped themselves from my father's signet ring onto the sealing wax of his confidential letters, and even appeared, their folded wings discreetly concealing their nakedness, on the boxes of Edinburgh rock sold in the village shop.

This shop was the centre of all the life of the village,

104

which, unlike an English village, had no pub. Anyone who wanted to meet anybody else did so in the shop, and as the owner resented having it jammed with non-buyers, people used to spread out their purchases as much as possible. The women who lived in the granite cottages of the village would drop in three or four times a day, buying first a small cube of lard, and then a bag of sugar, following this up with an ounce of tea and perhaps, if there was some bit of gossip that they particularly wanted to spread, by the purchase of a halfpenny stamp, for a railed-off corner served also as a post office. A bell tinkled each time the door was opened, and if one was waiting outside, the opening door let out not only the sound of the bell but also a delicious smell compounded of soap, brown sugar, lamp oil, cheese, lead pencils, boiled sweets, binder twine, Indian tea, boot polish, cocoa, and Elliman's embrocation.

Apart from the main shop, there were only two other stores in the village. One belonged to the baker, who, in addition to making the bread for the neighbourhood, cooked many of the Sunday dinners. The wives left joints of meat at his store on their way to the kirk, and he put them in his bread oven; an hour of the service followed by half an hour of sermon saw even the biggest joint done to a turn, ready to be carried home for the meal.

The third store belonged to the shoemaker. In his low-roofed workshop he sat crouched over the iron lasts, teaching his son how to shape uppers and soles, to hammer and stitch and polish. The villagers' Sunday shoes might come from a factory in the south, but the ones they wore on weekdays grew, like much of their food, right under their eyes.

The people who lived on the outlying farms and who could not easily get to the shops had their needs met by the 'fleein' pedlar', a wizened old man who drove a caravan filled with merchandise. He had lined the inside of the van with shelves,

105

on which were stacked all kinds of goods. Broomheads and balls of string and bags of knitting wool hung from the roof, jars of brightly-coloured sweets were wedged upright between sacks of lentils and dried beans, and spools of sewing thread were tucked down between packets of canary seed and throat lozenges. Lengths of checked gingham and flower-printed calico stood upright in the corner, surrounded by tins of scouring powder and bars of cheeselike yellow soap; hairpins and celluloid combs nestled beside rat poison and corn solvent.

Occasionally, the pedlar invited me to go with him on his rounds. I was never quite sure that I ought to accept his invitation, because although life in the country was so safe for children that they could — and did — accept lifts from total strangers, trips with the pedlar were such fun that I felt sure that, if I asked permission, someone in authority would find a reason to forbid them. So I simply took a chance on not being found out, and clambered quickly into the back of his van.

Travelling in the van was like being inside a shaken-up kaleidoscope. As it jolted its way over the rough roads, the stock on the shelves jumped and revolved, rattling and changing colour as first one side of a tin and then the other came to the front. Half deafened by the clatter of the galvanized buckets and basins and washbowls that hung on the outside of the van, I sat precariously in the back doorway, sucking a yellow-and-green lollipop and enjoying the sight of the road reeling away behind. I welcomed the pedlar's gift of the lollipop, for, although it would only have cost me twopence, my weekly pocket money was threepence, and of this one penny had to be put in the church collection. The remaining two pennies I could spend as I liked, provided I saved enough to buy Christmas and birthday presents; the twopence was rarely available for sweets.

Present-giving, on this budget, called for much

ingenuity. Several weeks before Christmas I would stake out a secret territory into which the other children could not come, and start to make presents. I mounted foreign stamps, steamed off my father's letters, for my brothers, hoping against hope that they were not ones already in their collections. I made needlebooks from scraps of flannel for my mother and sisters, and peppermint creams — icing sugar mixed with essence and white-of-egg — for my governess. Everything had to be constructed with minimum of outlay, and I grew adept at annexing apparently useless trifles that grown-ups discarded. Did I spy a pearl button on the worn-out shirt with which the chauffeur was polishing the car? I ran for my scissors — it was just what I needed to fasten a needle-book. Did nobody want that magazine in the waste-paper-basket? The picture on the cover would make a lovely calendar, stuck on cardboard, a laboriously hand-written list of dates attached below by a length of coloured knitting wool. Once the sister nearest to me spent weeks secretly making a wardrobe for the clothes of my doll, Cuddly. She contrived it from a cardboard grocery-box, carefully painted to look like wood, with matchbox drawers, boot-button handles, and a looking-glass made from flattened silver paper. It was a present that I greatly treasured.

Perhaps it was just as well that we led a rather isolated life, because when we did visit other children I was always amazed at the variety and newness of their toys. Even if our parents had been hard up it would only have needed the sale of some small valuable from a room but rarely entered to have given us children not only the new bicycles for which we yearned (ours were only prevented from falling apart by much diligent maintenance-work carried out — under the direction of my elder brother — in a gloomy woodshed) but also many other longed-for delights. My parents paid so little attention to their smaller possessions that many were not even dis-

107

played; once, when a member of the royal family was coming to tea, my father suddenly had the idea that it might be nice to add to the decoration of the rooms through which she would pass and, rummaging in one of the safes, unearthed a few dozen 'objets de virtu'. He went from room to room, distributing these on suitable table-tops; my mother, the overlapping front of her tartan skirt held up like an apple-picker's apron, tiptoed round behind him, collecting them up again: the expected visitor, a discerning antiquarian, had the reputation of expressing such warm admiration of things that caught her eye that the owners would be left with little alternative but to offer them to her as gifts.

But although they were by nature generous, my parents would never have considered selling so much as an unused snuff-box to buy playthings for their children. Children, everyone agreed — everyone, that is, but the children themselves, who were not consulted — should not be brought up to think that life was easy.

Nobody seemed to find it incongruous that, while imposing this financial discipline on his children, my father himself travelled as casually to the Rockies to hunt bear, or to Norway to fish for salmon, as he did to the next county to shoot grouse. He bought his cigarette-cases at Asprey's, his London suits in Savile Row, and was as much at home in St. James's Street as he was on the moors. My mother's jewelry was dazzling; she couldn't possibly wear it all at once and was occasionally agreeably surprised to find, tucked into a drawer of a jewel-case, a sapphire bracelet or pair of diamond earrings that she had, in her gentle, unworldly way, forgotten that she possessed.

My father was never ostentatious. Normally, he wore little of value except for a gold watch and chain and a signet ring, and although he was fussy about his stockings — he would never wear any that had been darned — his daytime clothes

108

were usually old. The blue and green of his hunting-tartan kilt was faded, and the collars of his shirts — already turned inside out by the servants — were worn through on the second side as well. His jackets, patched on the elbows with squares of leather, sported darns on the lapels, where barbed fishing flies had been temporarily parked and overhastily withdrawn.

He did, however, keep a tidy tweed jacket — with buttons made from intricately-twined leather thongs — to wear on formal occasions, and his scarlet evening kilt, venerable rather than old, was always impeccably pleated. As well as the jackets he was then wearing, he still had the khaki one that he had worn at the battle of Festubert, in the 1914–18 war, when he had so very nearly lost his arm. Blackened with blood, this hung in a glass-fronted cupboard in the billiard-room, next to the satin coat of my great-great-great-grandfather, who had been the unwitting cause of women first being allowed to enter the Houses of Parliament. A Member of Parliament, this ancestor had been entrusted with a fund set up for widows, and had handled it so unskilfully that when he was finally taken to task, some of the women who had suffered from his maladministration were allowed into the Chamber — previously barred to females — to listen to his arraignment.

Whether it was trying on this and other ancient jackets to see if we had yet grown as tall as our ancestors, or launching cockerels — suitably fortified with whisky-soaked grain — off the top of the tower, to discover if their barnyard upbringing had deprived them of the ability to fly, there was always something to be interested in, some new thing to do. But we also did particularly pleasant things again and again. About once a year, for instance, we climbed the volcano-shaped mountain that dominated the whole estate. Riding the seven miles to the foot of the mountain, we left our ponies at a farm and, on foot, started the ascent. For the first two miles, the path wound through forests; then, coming out above the tree line, it continued over a section of grouse moor. Cartridges, their scarlet cardboard covers disintegrating among the brown heather roots, lay scattered around the abandoned turf butts, where the guns had been concealed during the previous shooting season, and far above us an eagle drifted silently, scanning the slopes for game. We stopped to drink at one of the small pools that, spring-fed, lay hidden in the gulleys scored down the side of the mountain, and the dogs, fended off until after we had drunk, plunged in and bathed as they lapped. Up and up we went, till the heather gave way to bare rocks; another couple of hundred feet and we were on the summit.

Here, in a circle around what had been, perhaps, the top of one of the northern hemisphere's last active volcanoes, lay the ruins of a prehistoric vitrified fort. Nobody knew how the builders had succeeded in fusing the stones together. One theory was that they had used alternate layers of wood and stone and then set fire to the wood, but this would hardly have generated enough heat to melt the granite. Who had built the fort, and why, and how they had done it was a mystery, but there in the sun, eating our picnic, we felt a close bond between ourselves and the vanished race that had shaped the stones on which we sat, as if we were part of them and they of us. When I grew up, I visited ancient ruins in other lands — Machu Picchu, the Pyramids, Angkor Wat — but I never felt this same sensation of kinship with the dead. The Incas and the ancient Egyptians and the Khmers were not my ancestors, and they had nothing to say to me. The Picts were, and had.

We dozed in the sun, brushing away the flies with wisps of bracken as idly we studied the view. From here, the entire estate was visible. Below and to the right lay the grouse

110

moors, purple in the afternoon sun; a livid gash on the shoulder of one moor marked the granite quarry, and close to it a rectangular clearing showed the position of the sheep dips. Fields of every shape and size, from the rough enclosures of the upland crofts to the lush, spreading pastures of the big farms in the valley, lay with all their secrets exposed to us, as if drawn on a map. Around them, like giant mufflers, coiled the dark coniferous forests, broken here and there by trails and by the stump-studded clearings of the foresters.

There, far below, was the village, the square tower of the kirk, which looked so tall when one stood in the square, seeming hardly higher than the roof of the shop. Nearby, the bakery chimney was sending a thin wisp of smoke straight up into the still air. From this height, the distant loch seemed like a tiny looking glass, and the single track of the railway resembled a piece of fencing wire left lying carelessly across the fields. Were those the cows going in to be milked, those creeping dots down there by the granite smudge of the Home Farm? And what was that shiny black beetle scurrying — pursued by an attenuated cloud of dust — along the road that led away to the sea? Yes, it must be the car, with the chauffeur at the wheel, off to fetch my mother from her regular visit to a tenant who, falling ill, had been whisked away to the hospital. We watched the car; it would, we knew, vanish from sight about the time it reached the far boundary of the estate, away on the horizon, where the river widened and grew sluggish as it entered the plain. Our eyes retraced the bright line of the river as far as the castle grounds.

There stood the castle — unchanging, protective. At that distance, it seemed like something remembered from a dream. From its slender flagpole, my father's standard — three gold crowns on a scarlet field — floated over the tower and turrets, the spiral stairs and secret rooms, showing

111

that he was at home, and very much in charge. Here at our feet was all our world; we belonged to it, and it to us.

My father died in 1931, when I was ten. He thought that he had arranged an income for my mother, should he die before her, but his lawyers had neglected to remind him to sign a vital document, and his two-page will resulted in my elder brother inheriting not only his title, the castle and the estate but also all his personal money. Hopelessly baffled by the complexities of the law, which might well — had her professional advisers been more diligent — have awarded her support, my mother resigned herself to providing for herself and her five other children out of the remnants of her dowry, itself greatly depleted by the sums that she had, with no thought for herself, spent on such things as restoring to the castle its missing heirlooms. Banished from the castle, she moved to London, where she rented a modest house in Chelsea, at that time unfashionable and cheap.

Overjoyed to find that in this small dwelling I was no longer either frightened or lonely — for I could call, from my tiny bedroom, to my mother in the drawing room — it never even occurred to me to regret the ending of my childhood in Scotland.